ALICE COOK

Atherton–Tales From a Lancashire Lass

First edition

Editing by John S Tantalon
Cover art by Rob Warden

This book was professionally typeset on Reedsy.
Find out more at reedsy.com

Contents

Foreword

Born Alice Eckersley, on the 21st of January 1915, at 13, Garden Place, Atherton Lancashire.

Alice was born into poverty and was one of nine children living in a two bedroomed house, but what always shone through was the love that she shared with her family. It was instilled in us all as children, family was the most important thing in life. I am 84 years old now and the love of my family is still the defining legacy that I would attribute to my mam.

When I think of my mam I think of a caring, loving person, our door was always open to friends and family.

During the war Alice took in evacuees, John and Joan, the love and care that was given to us, as her own children, was shared with them. This was plain to see when twenty years later John arrived at the door with a smile on his face.

Alice was always there to give anyone a helping hand when needed, be it family, friends and neighbours. She became the spokesperson for the underdog. She fought for wage slips to be issued at the 'John Bullougher Nut and Bolt Works' in Bag Lane, Atherton, she encouraged everyone to join the union, she stood for fairness and equality. She was political and a forward thinker.

I reflect that so many of Alice's grandchildren and great-grand children have now gone to university, and how proud she would have been. Alice was a clever, articulate and self-educated woman. She was born before her time. University was something that Alice would have snatched the opportunity to attend with both hands; she would have excelled and soared.

If ever there was a medical emergency in the neighbourhood, then it was my mam and dad who everyone turned to, from fishhooks stuck in lips, to chip pan oil that had fallen on a child's head, my mam and dad were the ones to deal with these traumatic events.

In later years this led on to Alice, at the age of forty-two, training to become a nurse. A training that she would eventually need to use when caring for my dad, when less than ten years later he was diagnosed with incurable cancer. My mam nursed and loved him, at home, until he took his last breath.

My mam lived until she was 99 years of age. For the last five years of her life, with the support of her entire family, she moved to Scotland, to live with my daughter, Alice's granddaughter, Shelagh, and her husband John. Here she was given the same care and love that she had given to Lambert. She died surrounded by her family, feeling the love that had always meant so much to her.

In October 2014, Alice was taken on her final journey home to be with Lambert, the love of her life – together again in Atherton.

Ann Patricia Hutson – Alice's Daughter

Acknowledgement

'Our' Gordon Cook
Ann Hutson

All of Alice's Family

Dedicated in Loving Memory

Lambert Cook
Sheila Hayley
Stanley Cook

Credits

Edited by John S Tantalon
Cover art and typesetting by Rob Warden
Arranged by Allan Scott

1958

When I first went to Atherleigh it was to work on the mentally handicapped children's ward as an auxiliary. Four of the children, Philip, Leslie, Mary Flanagan and Julie had hydrocephalous (water on the brain). They seldom had visitors, Julie died and was buried one Christmas Eve in a communal grave in Atherton Cemetery – her only mourners being the staff who had loved and cared for her.

A couple of years ago, in the late 90s a doctor gave orders that a badly deformed child at birth should not be given any sustenance and be allowed to die. True compassion would have given a sleeping draught, just a little to ease the passing.

A Certain Corner Shop

Long since demolished, it stood on the corner of Mealhouse Lane and George Street, and most of the customers came from rows of terraced houses in Mealhouse Lane, Swan Street and Spring Gardens. It was the business of Mr Stringer: his wife and daughters serving behind the counter- buxom Nellie (the mainstay of the business) pale Polly and plump, quiet Mrs Stringer.

I'm reverie once more it takes form- the ping of the bell as ones fingers pressed the brass door latch to open the door to Aladdin's cave and my nostrils twitch at the thought of those pungent smells which once assailed them- the vinegar barrel with its wooden tap where, for a penny one could get ½ pint of chip appetizer' or, two pennorth of pickled onions from the large jar on the shelf above it!

The large block of crumbly Lancashire cheese which had a bite that matched its coluthe large barrel of black treacle measured out into your own jar or mug. Large blocks of butter, margarine or Kilverts lard, none pre-packed but weighed into nice oblong blocks by the wooden paddles wielded by Nellie!

Rolls of bacon, ham and a new modern bacon slicer.

Large sacks of sugar and flour weighed and packed at the time of purchase on the large scales on a shelf behind the counter! Unwrapped. unsliced bread. All around were shelves with a medley of contents.

Hanging on the walls behind the counter, like so many 'old Masters', were cards on which were attached various medications to cure the ills of the day, held in place by fine string or elastic thread. Little round boxes of Doan's backache and kidney pills (turns your urine green), "Bile Beans' and Beecham's pills for constipation. Small bottles of castor oil, always taken at the onset of labour to quicken the birth (given in orange juice or whisked in milk). Camphorated oil- good old standby- warmed, then rubbed on the chest its soothing vapours inhaled by anyone suffering from Bronchitis or any chest complaint.

Raspberry vinegar and olive oil for whooping cough: Liquafriuta a cough syrup smelling of garlic, which for a time was claimed by the makers to cure consumption! Ellerman's Rub for sprains or muscular or joint pains. fennings cooling powders' for teething or febrile babies.

Double E' teething powders. Hanging from the roof, long, narrow, sticky ribbons of fly catchers, dead flies adhering like so many currants on a sticky bun. In the window- a child's paradise- jars of sweets- 'Dolly Mixtures', wine gums, cocoanut mushrooms, Jap nuggets, 'Uncle Joes Mint Balls', trays of caramel, treacle toffee and raspberry toffee sprinkled with cocoanut. Id Fry's chocolate cream bars, thin bars of Cadburys chocolate, packet of dark shag, shredded cocoanut coated cocoa powder and-Toys for all seasons, shuttlecocks and paddles, whips and tops, skipping ropes, coloured marbles and glass alleys.

Books- two penny paperbacks- the fairy stories- Cinderella, Jack and the Beanstalk, the Three Bears, the Princess and the Bea, but- one had to belong to a more affluent family to afford two pence, after all, one only got a Friday penny and the sweets were very tempting.

In one corner of the window were sheets of straight pins, packets of sewing needles, reels of cotton, balls of darning wool, tins of 'Brighten Up', boot polish and in the opposite corner, apples and oranges. In the counter draw, packets of cigarettes- 'Senior Service, *Capstan', 6d for ten, but most popular Wild Woodbines', 2d for five' bought by weedy youths from their scant pocket money.

Coils of thick or thin twist tobacco, cut and weighed as required on the brass, counter scales, usually in % ozs, some of it to be chewed by miners when working underground.

Penny clay pipes for grandfathers. The customers, besides the children and youths, women with shauls draped over careworn shoulders, holding firmly in their grasp the 'Belly Bible', the book on which credit was entered, to be paid each Friday, payday, but obtaining free- all the local gossip- who is pregnant, given birth, sick or maybe died.

Food for the stomach, mind and tongue, all adding colour to grey drab lives. On the counter the large 'tally book' with Friday the day of reckoning; the day on which, like judgement day, all must be taken into account. The 'Corner Shop' where people met, shopped, talked, smiled, laughed, gone like the passing years and sadly soon to be forgotten.

Ancoats Hospital E.N.T (circa 1933)

Even today after almost 60years I can still remember the smell of those warm, moist, linseed poultices which my mother slapped under my jaws in an effort to reduce the swelling there; also, the taste of the castor oil, a dose of which, seemed to be the usual treatment for many childhood illnesses at that time.

I remember biting my mother's finger as she tried to push a desert spoonful down my throat whilst a neighbour held me in her grasp.

My sister has a school photograph of me, with my pale straw like hair pulled back by a white ribbon, and a beaming smile on a face with obviously swollen jowls; I must have been 8 or 9. years old at the time. As I was not seen by any doctor at the time, the illness was never diagnosed - mumps? T.B. glands? There are five of us, my two sisters and two brothers on the photographs, but I was the only one who seemed to get this swelling.

When I was about 11-12 years old, I had an infection of the tongue - a large yellow pustule in the centre. My Mother bought glycerine and borax from the chemist, and this was applied to my tongue to clean it but without success. She then took me to a local chemist (a Mr. Robinson) who after examining my tongue and asking my age, gave Mother a small packet of white powder which I was to take before retiring that night.

When I awoke the following morning, the result was amazing, there was no longer any sign of the infection, and as far as I can remember, I had no further trouble involving my mouth or throat 'till I was 18 years old.

One Saturday evening in September 1933 my boyfriend and I went to the Belle Vue Speedway in Manchester, where we had a drink in the bar; the glass of port I had, seemed to burn my throat at the time, and, a few days later I'd developed a sore throat and what appeared to be a small ulcer on one of my tonsils.

As the ulcer spread, swallowing became painful and difficult but in no way was my appetite affected and I continued to take a normal diet.

The affected tonsil now had the appearance of a piece of fungus, the shape was so distorted; my breath was offensive and now there was a discharge from my throat.

On the outside my neck was swollen on the inside the infected tonsil felt hot and dry, so my mother got me a tin of Vaseline, the contents of which, I placed a little at a time on my tongue to slowly dissolve and hopefully to find it's way onto the offending tonsil.

Home remedies failing I eventually visited the family G.P. who arranged for my attendance at the E.N.T. Hospital in Manchester the following day, where I was examined by the consultant Mr. Diggle.

He made the necessary arrangements for a chest x-ray to be taken at Ancoats Hospital the following day, Friday, then the following Monday I was admitted as an in-patient for the removal of one tonsil by diathermy.

I was admitted to the ward on Monday morning and, on Tuesday morning I was taken down to theatre, where in an ante-room, before the administration of an anaesthetic, my chest was wrapped in a folded wet sheet and over this was placed a sheet of tin foil. Now ready for the theatre, the mask was placed over my face and the nauseating smell of ether robbed me of consciousness.

Returned to the ward where, for the first couple of days I felt really ill, but this didn't last long and soon I was once again starving hungry.

During the illness I had never lost my appetite within three or four weeks was back at work, but, three months later the remaining tonsil developed the same distressing symptoms.

Back to Ancoats to see Dr.Diggle again where he explained his reason for not removing this tonsil along with the other. There had been the risk of haemorrhage with the first tonsil, and the second one was clear of infection at the time.

Thus, ins December I was admitted for the removal of the remaining tonsil by? caustic aci, so, no wet sheet or tin foil this time, but the obliging anaesthetist applied a few drops of oil of oranges to the mask when I told him the smell of ether nauseated me. Before being anaesthetized I also asked if it was possible for me to have a peep into the theatre where the operation was to take place.

He said this was an unusual request and "customers" weren't usually so interested in their surroundings, just eager to be back in the ward a soon as possible, the ether providing the oblivion of any proceeding's meantime. This "customer" happened to be very inquisitive and I was longing to know what was going on in the theatre at the other side of those big doors, so I asked, "If you were to be one of the principal characters in a play, wouldn't you like to see the stage and the rest of the cast before the performance? whereupon he went to the doors, opened one, peeped in, had a quick word with someone inside, then with a flourish opened wide both door. I don't really know what I expected to see, but all I did see was the unconscious figure of a man with a bandaged head, being transferred from the operating table to a trolley alongside, then the doors were closed, and, in a few minutes, the overpowering smell of ether dispersed the fragrance of the oil of orange, then I knew no more 'till I returned to the ward.

An uneventful recovery, then reporting back to the family G.P. Dr Lockwood, who said he had been informed by Dr Jessie of the T.B.Clinic that I should have been referred to him and not the E.N.T. Hospital. Dr Lockwood told me I was his patient, and he knew what was best for me!

I have in my possession a letter signed by "Herbert J. Dufforne" General Supt. & Secretary of Ancoats Hospital. dated 8.9 33 asking me to arrange a contribution towards the cost of my treatment as I was not a Manchester resident or subscriber. The average cost for each patient being £3-9-5 (approx. £3.47) weekly.

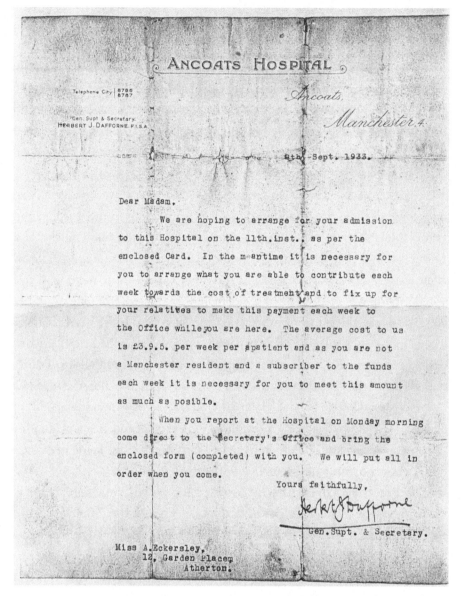

ANCOATS HOSPITAL

Telephone City | 8786
8787

Gen. Supt & Secretary.
HERBERT J. DAFFORNE, F.I.S.A.

Ancoats,
Manchester, 4.

8th Sept. 1933.

Dear Madam,

We are hoping to arrange for your admission
to this Hospital on the 11th.inst., as per the
enclosed Card. In the meantime it is necessary for
you to arrange what you are able to contribute each
week towards the cost of treatment and to fix up for
your relatives to make this payment each week to
the Office while you are here. The average cost to us
is £3.9.5. per week per patient and as you are not
a Manchester resident and a subscriber to the funds
each week it is necessary for you to meet this amount
as much as posible.

When you report at the Hospital on Monday morning
come direct to the Secretary's Office and bring the
enclosed form (completed) with you. We will put all in
order when you come.

Yours faithfully,

Gen.Supt. & Secretary.

Miss A.Eckersley,
12, Garden Place,
Atherton.

Copy of letter from Ancoats Hospital regarding costs of treatment there in 1933

Atherleigh Hospital

When I was nursing on night duty on a geriatric ward,
Awakening the patients at 6am for toileting many times I've heard
"I wish I was dead" by patients old and weary and tired of life

Men and women who had worked in the mills, the mines, the steel works
Awakened in early morning by the "Knocker up"
With the wire tipped pole, rattling on the bedroom window
Making sure one was in time for work.

Patient (and staff) outing

Alice outside Atherleigh after its closure (1990)

The only surviving building "The Nursery" when Atherleigh was the workhouse

Union offices where people went for "Poor Relief" in the days of the workhouse

When this was the workhouse laundry, inmates provided most of the workforce

Atherleigh

❦

After the Second World War the Socialist Government took away the stigma of the Workhouse' (formerly in England), an institution maintained at public expense. where able-bodied paupers did unpaid work in return for food and accommodation.

Through the gates entered the old, the sick. the orphans and the inadequate to be fed. clothed and sheltered.

The Workhouse was the last refuge of the young woman expecting an illegitimate child. They would be parted, the child to the nursery and the sother to the female section where she would be allotted work in one of the departments - the laundry. the kitchens, domestic work on the wards etc.

Considerable heartache must have been caused on admission of aged couples by their separation, the man to the male section and the woman. man to the female section. At the porter's lodge. overnight accommodation was provided for vagrants:

They were given food a bath and a bed. For this they were expected to do some menial job, such as chopping firewood, delivering coal or coke to the wards etc. After one night they had to move on to the next town.

The sons of aged parents were expected to contribute to their maintenance, even if only a few shillings weekly.

Many Workhouses grew their own vegetables and the one later known as Atherleigh Hospital cultivated some surrounding fields and also reared pigs.

The Workhouses were modernised, and geriatric hospitals slowly came into being. places where the elderly, sick and infirm retained their dignity.

Gradually the high-sided cot-beds were disposed of and. instead of the usual practice of closing off the ward by putting a screen across the doorway during the bedpan round. each bed was given curtains on rails. thus, providing patients privacy whilst toileting.

Then patients were given weekly pocket money to buy sweets and toiletries from the WVS trolley. and newspapers and cigarettes from the newsagent who called daily on each ward.

Later a dress allowance was given so that each patient could have their own modern clothing. Other amenities were introduced. physiotherapy. occupational therapy. chiropody. carpeted day rooms with comfortable chairs and coloured TVs. A League of Hospital Friends bought hairdressing equipment, also a coach with facilities for wheelchairs and patients for outings during summertime.

Whilst no-one likes to leave their home in their final years, no longer was one haunted by the thought of the Workhouse'. One was assured of professional care when one was too debilitated to cope on one's own.

Alas, during Mrs Thatcher's term of office all this was changed, and the Health Service (once Britain's pride) began the changes which altered the whole concept of a cruelly National Service.

Atherleigh Hospital (formerly the workhouse) which had provided excellent services for geriatric and psycho-geriatric patients as well as a laundry service for Leigh Infirmary and Astley Hospital. was completely demolished in 1991.

The National Health Service Trust, Chief Executive at the time Dr Sandygradbrook (his doctorate is. I believe, in building not medicine), and when plans of a new General Hospital were talked of. I'm afraid we believed it! There are yet no signs of this being built!

Due to falling numbers of geriatric patients (in this day and age???)

Atherleigh could be demolished, and future patients accommodated in the new General Hospital (so we suckers presumed).

Now Leigh Infirmary laundry is being sent miles away to be laundered since privatization: soiled linen once done locally at Atherleigh has been done in various places as each private laundry fell down on the job. some even losing linen!

In December 1991 when I was attending Leigh Infirmary Outpatients Clinic.

a member of staff told me that she laundered her own uniform because they were only returned once a month by the present laundry. Soiled linen. once laundered at source. is now travelling miles through many towns: heaven help us if ever there is any kind of an epidemic!

There is a lot of 'pie in the sky concerning care in the community and the increasing number of elderly people and their care: aushroom growths of Homes for the Elderly meanwhile, there are - no physia, no occupational therapy, no mental stimuli, no League of Friends just an easy chair and a tele to boggle the mind.

Now we realize that the Health Service has engaged into duty to the elderly nick by packing their responsibility on to the Social Senice,

" "Residential Homes", could not afford to care for the Elderly Sick, they couldn't afford to with the new set aute farcilities & the added exporcle of muting care.

We elderly folk deserve some consideration we were here when the country needed us in the Second World War

Atherton

The mills, the mines, the steel works all gone from this once busy little town.

Forgotten in the drab wearying toil, the dangers and mostly for a pittance of
a wage – the workers educated for work and not for leisure
Found idleness unbearable.

Case History from a T.B Patient (1931)

This is a case history with a difference - it is written by the patient and relates to an experience of fifty years ago

It was all brought to mind when I read an article in the Leigh Journal of 26th February 1981 from their files of fifty years ago.

"Large numbers of workers could not afford to stay off work even though they were too ill to work. Insured people were going to work with temperatures of 101 degrees because they could not survive on 15 shillings (75p) per week sick pay"

My father was an invalid and at the time was in receipt of only half the above benefit, so my wages from the age of fourteen when I started work were an essential part of the family income.

Wages and working conditions for the majority of the workers were poor, but I digress: this is a case history, not a social history.

My health had been deteriorating for several months now. Each evening after returning home from work I would have my meal and immediately prepare for bed, sometimes as early as 7 p.m., but on awakening the following morning at 7a.m. felt neither rested or refreshed and I had no energy.

I had no appetite and had lost weight; I also seemed to be suffering from a kind of adolescent rickets- the bones of both my ankles and knees appeared enlarged, and when walking, stepping on or off the pavement, very painful, and climbing stairs daunting.

At the age of 16years 8 months in September 1931, I had my first period. On the first morning I vomited a large amount of bile and, for the next 10 days my period loss was heavy.

I had no further periods until the following January 1932, 4 months later, but in the meantime, I had surgery.

On the morning of November 24th, 1931, I got up to go to work after a restless night. I was immediately violently sick and had severe abdominal pain. I insisted on going to work, telling my mother I could probably "work it off", realising the loss of a day's wage meant adding to the family's financial burden.

I worked for approximately 2 hours, when 1 of my colleagues showed some concern at my pallor and realising, I was ill, took it on himself to ask the foreman if I could go home. I had to make my own way home, approximately 3 quarters of a mile away, and as I walked, I had to keep stopping whenever the pain became severe, so my progress home was slow as well as painful.

I duly arrived home, where my mother immediately put me to bed and gave me medication a Feenamint (an aperient) and some Indian Brandy.

She believed the bile I had vomited that morning was due to constipation thus an aperient was indicated; the Indian Brandy) was to warm my tummy and ease the pain!!!

It wasn't long before the medication became effective and I began the weary trot to the outside 'loo' the effect of the Feenamint then back into bed, to lean out over the side of the bed to vomit into a bowl whenever the 'snake in my tummy twisted and stretched' causing pain and nausea.

No sending for the doctor that was only done in cases of serious illness!! No Mother would take me to the evening surgery of the gamily GP.

At last, I was being examined by the family doctor, Dr Saunders, and I felt none of the apprehension and shyness usually felt by me on the very few visits I had ever made to the surgery, only a sense of relief, and faith in his ability.

His diagnosis was 'probably appendicitis, but there could be another cause anyhow, he would arrange for my immediate admission into hospital'.

I was to go straight home, and he would arrange for the local ambulance to convey me from there to B.R. Infirmary in the next town.

I was taken to the Casualty Department on arrival. after examination, transferred to Nicholson Ward, a Florence Nightingale type ward - 2 long rows of beds and a coal fired stove in the centre.

Here I was prepared for theatre by 2 nurses, only the nightlights were on and as they worked, they chatted about their hospital exam, results and both had apparently failed them. This meant they could no longer stay at their present hospital after failing the exams, which had followed a 12-month probationary period.

I remember shivering as they chatted away, blanket bathing then swabbing my abdomen with lotions before bandaging in readiness for transfer to the theatre and surgery.

Although ill, I was excited and inquisitive and, as I was wheeled on a stretcher into an anti-room alongside the theatre, could hear the clatter of instruments and the gay chatter of nurses and an atmosphere of great activity all around.

I had no idea what to expect when a young woman wearing a skirt and jumper entered, I thought she was the porter's wife, even when she began to administer the anaesthetic - chloroform. - but I had complete confidence in her.

The next thing I remember was struggling as 4 people in white held me down, then I seemed to be outside my body watching as they bent over me.

I returned to consciousness in the 5 bed Recovery Ward, and over my tummy I thought there was a cage with light bulbs in it. At my side was a staff nurse busily inserting needles in my breasts for the administration of a subcutaneous drip. I remember her saying, "Drat, the needle's broken in," - I wasn't aware of being hurt, only too tired to care.

The following morning our family G.P. who had been responsible for my admission the previous evening, came to see me, I asked if he thought I'd be fit enough to resume work in 3 weeks' time that would be "2 weeks here and a week's convalescence"

- then earning again.

He reassured me and I believed him. I know I was burning up with fever; he must have thought I was delirious as well I wasn't, I really believed it possible.

I remember the sheer bliss of lying there: no weary trudge to work.

I also remember the burning fever, the terrible thirst which even penetrated sleep dreaming always of water, seeing a water hydrant in the road, only to discover the water which issued forth from its spout was full of wooden splinters.

Another dream, another road, another hydrant, this time surrounded by a pile of dead fish over which I trod, only to find to my horror this time the water was full of fish scales.

Craftily asking for mouth washes when nurses were busy and watching as the water poured from the sink tap into a glass, instead of the nurse getting a glass of the usual pink mouthwash.

The sheer bliss of swallowing some of this wonderful liquid as I made a show of swishing it around my mouth, then spitting it out into a receiver - minus my illicit gulps.

My first oral fluids were a small amount of water every 3 hours and brandy, sugar and water approximately every 4 hours.

I even asked Matron for water when she made her daily round - accepted her statement, 'girly you are getting all the fluid you need from the drip', but she never gave me the reason why it should be administered; thus, besides, the fluid she was referring to felt like a solid block resting on my chest.

I remember pushing my feet out of bed to cool them and the little dark-haired Welsh nurse who scolded me each time she caught me.

Pleading for the window above my bed to be opened to let in the cold November air, thinking this would cool the fire that seemed to be burning me up.

My abdomen was cut in the centre mid-line from the pubic area to just above the naval, a 2nd wound was a typical appendix incision to the right of this.

The centre wound had stitches as well as metal clips; the appendix 1,8 clips.

The dressings were held in place by a many-tailed bandage, but my abdomen was very swollen and purple-looking, and I could only lie with my posterior on a rubber air-ring and seated in Fowler's position; on no account could I lie on my sides or make any sideways movement as my tummy seemed full of lead and with any sideways movement the weight moved too.

I developed a racking cough and a pain in my chest. Pneumonia was diagnosed and treatment with Kaolin poultices to both right and left thoracic regions was ordered. Over these another many tailed bandage to keep them in position, the Pneumonia 'jacket' of gamgee.

My only clothing at this time was a type of flannel bed jacket and a pair of knee-length theatre socks.

I also had a small, infected pressure sore on my tail bone. This also was poulticed, and a T-bandage applied. Thus, my entire trunk was bandaged. To add insult to injury, my right foot began to turn, owing to the pressure of bed linen, but prompt action soon put this right a cradle over my feet and a little gentle massage applied.

The 3 weeks I was in this ward I was on the free list that is, dangerously ill, but actually I felt in heaven. Just to lie there with all the indignity of total nursing care; a very painful, swollen abdomen, which I tried to hold each time I coughed up (what appeared to work - ah! Sheer bliss.

The 1st few days following the operation had a kind of unreality and I had only a vague awareness of the occupants of the other 4 beds.

Hearing the patient in the bed opposite praying for death and denying the existence of any God for refusing her release from soul-destroying pain,

She had been the victim of a road accident and received terrible injuries and her family were constantly by her bedside. Her husband bathed my hands and forehead with her cologne, in the midst of his trouble he had noticed my need. I've no memory of her death, just a vague impression of an empty bed and strange silence.

The lady in the opposite corner bed, whose gallstones were 'enough to pave the streets of Bolton' - she vanished in the same way.

The other 2 patients were a 47-year-old married woman with a family of 7 children who had had a hysterectomy, and a spinster in her early 50's who had a colostomy.

My mother visited me daily and although I longed for these visits, I just couldn't keep awake. It seemed too big an effort to keep my eyes open -

speaking was exhausting with intermittent coughing, and, once the fever had subsided, the terrible sweating.

Once I was taken off the drip, I was given gradually increasing amounts of oral fluids and the brandy, sugar and water continues for several more days at 3 or 4-hourly intervals; now each morning around 10am I was given a glass of egg, milk and brandy and I remember once complaining because the flavouring had been left out of my drink. This caused much hilarity amongst the staff and 1 staff nurse teased me and nick named me 'Brandy Face'.

Although I was given frequent mouth washes and oral hygiene, my mouth felt as dry as a cinder track; with no saliva flow to moisten my food and no appetite, I could not summon any enthusiasm for the special diet prepared for me - steamed fish, tripe cooked in milk, egg custard and other nourishing, easily digested, unappetising foods.

I just could not summon the energy or interest to eat - I only wanted water - gallons, if I could get it - and sleep. The staff pleaded, threatened and eventually told my mother to tell me I would die if I continued to refuse nourishment. Somehow, I didn't seem able to make them understand - I didn't like milk! - Only in tea why I only took the egg and milk because Sister insisted, and I was too polite to deny the voice of authority - besides the 'flavouring' was in a glass of its own. • (Brandy)

Panic stations - I couldn't P.U. - Sister took a quick look at my big purple tummy and a gentle tap, anxious looks, then a dose of lemon-flavoured medicine (? pot cit) followed shortly by a 'good result'.

My only other medicines were a foul-tasting expectorant for my cough (I managed somehow to gather the information it contained Tincture of Belladonna) and liquid paraffin, the latter was evidently the cause of all the yellow, smelly, oil stains on my air-ring cover and draw sheets.

Three weeks of first-class care and then the transfer to a newly built ward 'Collin Cooper' - but my mother would not be allowed her daily visits - just Wednesday, Saturday and Sunday.

Anyhow I was now taking an interest in life again. I could even read a paragraph from a newspaper or a book without forgetting each consecutive word as I read it (this actually happened the first time I tried to read just before leaving Recovery Ward - my mother had brought a couple of weeklies to try to stimulate my interest in something).

I was even allowed to sit in a wheelchair on the veranda a few hours daily.

Then I developed an appetite, I was ravenous, but now in this ward, was given the normal hospital diet of the time.

At breakfast and teatime only bread and butter and cups of tea were provided, but staff would boil an egg if the patient had one.

The only real meal of the day at mid-day consisted of 2 courses - the main course usually a hash of meat and potatoes, followed by a sweet- always a milk pudding - rice or sago. A mid-morning drink and a supper time drink also were provided, but nothing more.

Patients' lockers usually held a supply of eggs, preserves, a little pot of butter, a bag of sugar and other things provided by relatives and friends to supplement the inadequate diet.

With the return of my appetite. on each visit my mother would bring home-made saucer pies and various tasty titbits, sent by friends and relatives. I seemed to have a bottomless stomach.

One supper time an Irish nurse gave me a cup of chicken broth. The pepper in it nearly stopped my breath, but to me it was delicious.

She had received a chicken from home and that evening the nurses had cooked in in the ward kitchen, probably unofficially.

I was the only patient this broth was given to, and I realize no, what a generous, kindly action it was, then I remember what a bony scarecrow I was at the time and how the staff had noticed my hunger.

Christmas - the carols early on Christmas morning by a choir of nurses in their cloaks and carrying candles. A surprise present at the foot of my bed when I awoke - it was a case containing a comb and mirror and had been bought from donations given by visitors into the collecting boxes at the entrance to the ward.

From friends and relatives, I had received chocolates, sweets and fruit - real luxuries to me, but I'd have swapped the lot for a 'chip butty'.

Taken by a nurse for a tour of the wards in my wheelchair - the children's ward, where in a cot near the stove was a tiny baby. The young parents, the only visitors in the ward, were alongside and I felt sad that they should be spending. This day in these circumstances.

Back to my ward and the only real meal of the year in any hospital at that time- Christmas Dinner not hash and milk pudding, but turkey, Christmas pudding and all the trimmings - and the mayor to carve the magnificent fowl.

Beautiful ward decorations made by the staff and, that evening, a concert given by them. In my mind's eye I see them now, remember the songs, the acts, but mostly the performers, girls who had nursed me and doctors who had responsible for treatments.

Visitors in the afternoon - my mother brought my 12-year-old sister in her first visit to see me - she stayed at the foot of the bed and wouldn't come near me, for I was merely a bag of bones with a pair of saucer-like objects for eyes and I knew my appearance scared her. I didn't feel hurt or insulted, somehow, I understood and realised the addition of a few stones in weight and our usual affectionate relationship would be resumed.

Christmas over and back to reality - the normal hospital routine and the inadequate hospital diet which was supplemented by my mother on 'visiting days'.

There was an incident during the doctor's round which had momentarily dismayed me, pausing at my bedside he turned to Sister and remarked, "We've had the results of the sputum tests - there is no trace of T.B." I had gone cold at the thought - T.B.! Not me why, I was getting better, and everyone knew you didn't get better from T.B., there was no known cure.

Whilst in Collin Cooper ward I remember a patient in the bed facing me who had gangrene of the womb. She was in her thirties, and I would say terminally ill. She had Snow-White bobbed hair, skin like alabaster, roses on her cheeks which only a high fever could produce.

She had a blood transfusion taken from her husband at her bedside.

He was a miserable-looking man who complained about her being in hospital. He though she should be at home looking after him and their 9-year-old son!

I was taken in a side ward in a wheelchair to cheer up a 15-year-old girl who had swallowed some straight pins whilst packing bolts of cloth in a weaving mill. She had to swallow balls of cotton wool.

My health continued to improve, and I was eventually transferred to Edmund Potter Convalescent Hospital, where there was a more relaxed atmosphere, and, more important to me, a more substantial diet.

As far as I remember there were 8 beds in this ward, and all were occupied by convalescing patients; the bed next to mine occupied by a young woman in her twenties suffering from 'fluid on her lungs'.

She had a hole in her back at the base of her lungs and, each morning, she would cough whilst a nurse held a receiver at the opening and fluid oozed out. This patient was ambulant. I do remember 1 screen in this ward, so I saw this treatment carried out in the mid-morning, the usual time for any dressings, etc.

I also remember the visit of a consultant, Dr Mothersoul, to a patient who had her left breast off and had received radium treatment.

The doctor, wearing a black frock coat and carrying a top hat was treated with great defence by the accompanying staff. The woman's chest was exposed and, as well as the breast amputation scar, below the armpit and under the shoulder-blade were several small marks, similar to a healing chicken pox. The woman later told me these marks were where radium seeds had been implanted??

My mother asked for my discharge explaining that the local Vicar had been able to arrange for my admission to a seaside convalescent home run by the Church. This was not true. Mother had made tentative enquiries and received some half-promises to see if something could be arranged; but she knew the day she took me home nothing had come of it. I suppose she found the bus or tram fare getting too much, and she had been coming visiting for weeks in the worst of wintry weather.

Besides, I was now ambulant, cheery, hungry, looking better than I had for months, even if I did have a swollen purple tummy and I could only go to sleep on my back with my knees bent. I was getting better.

At home my mother explained the cause of my illness- a large mass of T.B. glands in the Caecum, this had been removed (some mention had been made of the transverse colon, but she hadn't quite understood this part of the statement) but I had developed Peritonitis and Pneumonia after the operation.

All this happened fifty years ago, before the use of antibiotics or modern technical aids, when hospitals were 'run on a shoestring' and every penny accounted for.

Financially dependent on the generosity of public benefactors and the general public, before the era of the National Health Service the modern Welfare State.

My mother attributed my recovery, partly to my love of life (I had always been the tomboy of the family) and also to her philosophy 'What has to live no frost can kill' and to the fact 'miracles do happen'.

My tribute is to the hospital staff of yesteryear whose skill and care made possible my recovery and gave me these bonus years.

My miracle came later - I had a family of my own: impossible after peritonitis???

By the way, I certainly didn't go convalescent. I had to go in a T.B. Sanatorium, but that's another story!

Christmas 1997

Memories of my Mother Sarah's Christmas'
'Tis Christmas once again and memory takes me back to when
I was a child many, many years ago. Once again, I'm in the living
room of my childhood home,
  secure, loved and never lonely.

I see my mother seated in her rocking chair, alongside the table with the light from the blue porcelain bellied lamp, shedding a kindly glow on her beloved face.

We children gathered around, some sat on the hearthrug in front
of the fire, some on the wooden settle and some on the rush
bottom chairs. Then she would tell of the Christchild's birth - her childhood Christmas memories how on Christmas morn, she and her brother and sisters went in their parents' bedroom to sing.

"Brightest and best of the suns of the morning, Dawn on our
darkness and lend us thine aid, Star of the East, the horizon adorning
Guide where our infant Redeemer is laid
Then tell us a poem from her childhood
"Twas the night before Christmas When all through the house.
Nothing was stirring, not even a mouse!"

Always without fail our favourite story "The Little Matchgirl". such a sad story, but the shooting star and the little girl being gathered in her grandmother's arms and carried to heaven away from the cold inhospitable world in which she had lived, made such a happy ending. We realised how fortunate we were, we had a happy home, loving parents and a wonderful mother.

Financially we were as poor as proverbial church mice, but such memories I have of my childhood are beyond price made possible by a wonderful Mother - Sarah.

Educating Alice

I know I may be long in the tooth to make a serious attempt at education, but when in my sixties, after a course of instruction at the local tech, I sat the exam, in O-Level English.

It was taken at the tech, college in the next town and the test commenced at 9.30am.

Everyone was seated at their desk and had filled in details of name, number and course taken, then dead on 9.30 am the referee announced, 'you may now commence'.

A rustle of papers, then a sort of pregnant silence, and, when I looked at the syllabus, I understood! You never saw such a load of old crap as the titles of those essays. Who the dickens had dreamt up that load of cods- wallop? Him! Must have been some old dry as dust professor playing 'silly buggers.

The essay on 'The trouble with my hair', for instance, who could write any kind of essay on that? Why, one paragraph would require three words- that of the bald man, thus 'I am bald', straight to the point and conveying all the necessary information.

Today I have changed my mind, Mike who gave a series of lectures on 'writing for pleasure and profit' said that, given a title on any subject and he could write a reasonable essay, so I've looked at the list again, and realise I'm the one at fault, not Professor X!

Trying to get a rusty brain in action again needs time and patience, so I've looked over the list again and realised the truth of Mike's statement. The difference is, I'm writing this in the comfort of my own home and in complete absence of stress, so, below is the story of——————-

The Trouble with my Hair

This is a brilliant idea for an essay! What changed my mind? Thinking about my crowning glory. It's grey now, cut rather short and permed, but by gum it's looked a mess in its time.

At birth, like my brothers and sisters I had dark brown hair, but this was soon superseded by snow-white hair. Stood on end giving me the appearance of an albino hedgehog.

I know this is true: I've seen the photograph taken at the local baby clinic when I was about eight months old and in my mother's arms. Don't worry in all other respects I was pretty and very pleasant.

One of the assistants at the clinic asked my mother why she hadn't named me 'Lily', for I was as fair as one! All the same I had a distinctive mop.

As I grew older my hair grew darker in colour and lengthened, every hair as straight as a piece of straw and just as attractive. In fact, if I'd been stuck in the middle of a field I'd have passed as a scarecrow, you'd have sworn I'd borrowed one of Worzel Gummidge's wigs!

Now my brothers had a very apt description for a 'hair do' like that, but one they'd never use when referring to my locks. After all, who'd say that their sister had a head of hair that looked like 'a sod over a rat hole!' Not them! They might tell me they'd 'seen better hair on bacon', but the S.O.R.H was the ultimate in insults and not for their sister. But you know, when I look back, I realise my hair must often have had that appearance.

My elder sister has a family group photo taken at school, of two of my brothers, two of my sisters, our niece and me - no mistaking me - swollen glands, mumps distorting my usual oval face, nevertheless a beaming smile and that thatch of pale straw pulled back from my forehead by a white ribbon.

Whether that photo confirmed the idea in my mother's mind, that 'something would have to be done with our Alice's hair', I don't know, but

31

from then on it was 'bobbed' and I sported a 'donkey fringe'. That is until my brother Jack took my hair in hand; he cut it but forgot I was a female and gave me a 'pudding cut'.

My Mother went mad at the result and made him take me to the barbers, where the barber cut a short fringe in front, after which he stood back, surveyed his handiwork (and our Jack's), and grunted 'S best I can do'. Thus, I no longer looked like a S.O.R.H, but more like a bleached coconut!

At last fashion took a hand. When I was thirteen years old the 'Elton Crop' became all the rage and now hairdressing salons (of a fashion) for females were opening. The wife of the barber who had attempted to improve on my unusual hair style had started ladies' hairdressing in the same premises as her husband.

A friend of mine decided the crop was for her, costing sixpence. (2 ½ p) it seemed a lot of money, but she had thick red course hair, which was, almost, not quite as unruly as mine - it was a success. It looked lovely, a bit boyish, but certainly a great improvement, and thus - my mother's eagerness to see if the same transformation could happen to me.

Never was a sixpence so well spent, I came out of that hair- dressers a different girl. The neat crop accentuated the oval shape of my face and the shingled effect on the bump at the back of my head had been done with such artistry, a sculptor would have been proud. Alas this style needed frequent trips to the hairdressers and sixpence was hard to come by, so my hair just had to grow.

The crop had somehow tamed my hair and made it more manageable so my hair could be neatly trimmed in the fashion of the 'bob' by one of my older brothers (not Jack of course) but in the meantime at the age of fourteen I had joined the army of the worker force of Lancashire and some of my workmates had curls and waves on which I cast envious eyes. Some of these had naturally curly hair, others had contrived to make curls and waves by artificial means using curling pins or curling or waving irons.

From Woolworths for sixpence (2 ½ p) one could buy a pair of metal curling tongues or a waving iron. By heating and using one of these one could have a head full of curls or a head of waves that resembled corrugated cardboard

(well mine did)

Many are the times I've overheated the curlers and many a bright curl finished up on the tongues instead of my head.

Ah well, before I'd burned the lot off, some wonderful magician invented 'the permanent wave', you know it needs someone as old and long in the tooth as me, to appreciate what it has done for the morale of the countless females who were born with a crowning glory that did as much for their ego as a fur hat in a downpour at Ascot.

After a perm, personalities changed, those wavy locks gave a boost to the plainest females, and they looked round for other beautifying aids and suddenly there were droves of ducks turning into swans.

This swan added a little auburn rinse to her locks- not much, but enough to give my curls colour as well as form.

Now this was ok until the war, when rinses were either difficult to obtain or beyond my means, so I decided to try a little 'Dolly cream'. This is used in laundering lace curtains and covers to give them a deep cream effect. It is made by the manufacturers of the 'Blue Bag' or 'Dolly Blue' which was used in the final rinsing water when laundering white linen or cotton goods.

I only used it once; once was enough, I could see shades of Worzel Gummidge coming back into my locks, so curtains and covers only were treated by 'Dolly Cream', afterwards.

Now you've an idea of 'the trouble with my hair', or should I say, 'the trouble I've had in the past with my hair' and looking at the coloured snapshot of my four grandsons and I taken at the eldest ones twenty first birthday party, you'd never believe that the elderly lady with the blue rinsed coiffured hair had ever sported a 'hair- do like the ones in the above essay!

This is the essay I should have written. Never mind, better luck next time.

Family group outside The Unitarian School (Chowbent). Back row-Sister Vera, Brother Ken and Alice. Front row-Brother Bill, Niece Irene and Sister Phylis (school photo)

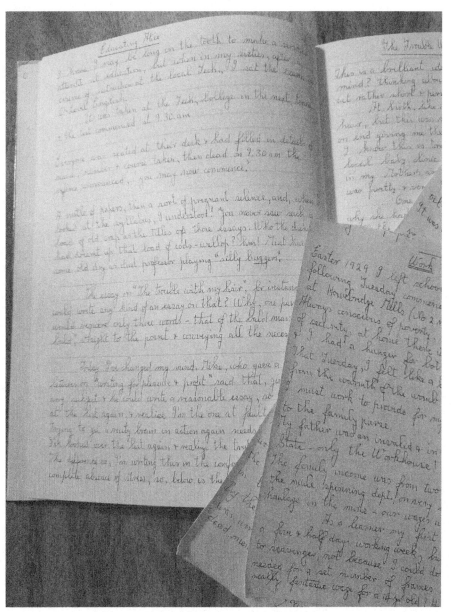

The original hand written copy of Educating Alice

Home

I was born at 8.45pm at 13 Garden Place, Atherton, the fourth house in a row of two-bedroom terraced houses. All five houses have now been demolished and car parking for Eckersley Precinct is now in their place.

I of times trod that cobbled pavement and remembered with affections the old house', two rooms up and two rooms down. On the table in the living room the beautiful paraffin lamp with its blue porcelain belly supported by figured brass on a cream stone base, the kind mellow light it shed, hiding the shabbiness of the furniture in this my home.

The old-fashioned fireplace where the iron kettle always seemed to be perched halfway on the living coals, ready for the favourite brew (Black and Greens) or for hot water to wash the dishes or other domestic chores.

Every Friday morning, my mother black leaded the entire fireplace and Brasso'd the fire irons and the fender, the fender and fire irons to be placed on the flock-bed of the sofa (actually it was a wooden settle). The flock bed was covered by a cotton tartan cover with a frilled base, the colours usually in reds and blues.

The fire irons were replaced in front of the fire on Saturday morning. Four rush bottomed chairs, a wooden rocker and an old-fashioned wooden dresser, on top of which, in pride of place in the centre, was the big leather backed family Bible which contained the names and dates of births of each member of the family.

In later years a horned gramophone shared pride of place with the family Bible, and in memory I hear once again Madam Patti singing "Home Sweet Home", the recording on one side of the disc only, the other side blank.

Count John McCormack, Dame Nelly Melba, Carouso, Tom Burk, Peter Dawson, Lotte Leyman (?), Paul Robeson and others as well as music by brass bands Wingates, Brigghouse and Rastrick, Bess o'the Barnes and Black Dyke from Deep Harmony to Colonel Bogey. Ballads, Gilbert & Sullivan light. operas, Negro Spirituals, aries and choruses from famous operas and on Sundays Handels Messiah, this was our family's interest. in music stimulated by records purchased by my elder brother Alf with his limited 'pocket money'.

I nearly forgot to mention the square wooden table, covered by a table oil cloth and in the centre our beautiful lamp. On Sundays at tea-time a white damask tablecloth covered the table oil cloth. The flag floors which had to be mopped and stoned (the wet floor scoured by a 'rubbing stone' and under the furniture), finished off with a smooth coating of 'donkey brand', the wet hand or mop wiped across the surface horizontally to give a professional finish.

When my sister Vera started work at the age of 14years (she was 2 years and 9 months my senior) she began to save her shilling pocket money to buy a coco-matting for the floor from Jack Lowes, ladies and gents outfitters, stockists of floors coverings, jewellery and one time pawn broker. From the market my mother purchased 'oil cloths' for the floor under the furniture -it was 'turkey red' patterned in red and blues, the coco-matting covered the rest of the floor.

In front of the fireplace a home-made rug from strips of material cut from worn out coats and pants and pegged into and opened washed, hessian sugar bag.

Suspended from the roof before the fireplace the line' four long wooden staves supported at each end in an iron bracket, with ropes attached to pulleys on the ceiling enabling the 'line' to be raised or lowered at will.

On washing days in bad weather, the wet clothes were hung on these lines to dry, but weekends the line was filled with the ironed laundry; with such pride (always your best and most attractive things on the front line).

None of your modern electric, steam irons or your modern easy to care materials; the ironing was by flat irons, or - as used in my home - a 'box' iron. This was a kind of boat shaped contraption, with a smooth flat bottom and a handle attached to a kind of lid, which, at the pressing of a knob could open further withdrawal of a cooling heater and the insertion of a red hot one just taken from the heart of the fire. A warm job in winter, but in the summer simply 'melting' for the 'ironer'.

On washing days in the winter as the day drew dark, the lamp was taken from the living room into the kitchen and a candle was lit in the living room, but the light from the fire also gave a glow as well as drying the wet laundry.

Outside 13 Garden Place, Atherton. Alice (centre) holding niece Joyce and her brother Stanley, Bill

Alice's mother and father Sarah and John George Eckersley and family at their golden wedding anniversary celebration at the The Railway Inn, Bag Lane, Atherton (children in this photo had lost their mothers)

Approx 1949-Back garden at 162 Devonshire Road, Atherton. Nephew Harry Parsonage visiting Atherton from Wellington, New Zealand. Joined by some of the family

Unexpected visitors

On Thursday week, Mr. and Mrs. J. G. Eckersley, 162, Devonshire-rd., Atherton, had three unexpected visitors. They were Mr. H. Parsonage, Assistant Director of Employment, New Zealand Labour Department, their nephew, who was accompanied by Mr. and Mrs. J. V. Brennon, chief migration officer, New Zealand Government in London.

Mr. H. Parsonage was the N.Z. delegate to the International Labour Conference at Geneva, from June 8th to July 2nd. He is now visiting England and Scotland before returning home via America on July 31st.

Mr. Brennon took a movie film of the re-union for Mr. Parsonage to take home to his parents.

They attended the Royal Garden Party at Buckingham Palace yesterday (Thursday).

Mr. Parsonage's parents emigrated from Atherton to New Zealand 36 years ago. His father is Mr. Ned Parsonage, who was employed at Gib Field Colliery. His mother was formerly Ann Eckersley, of Howe Bridge. Also in New Zealand are his uncles, Chris and Bill Parsonage, who emigrated at the same time.

Newspaper cutting about the visit

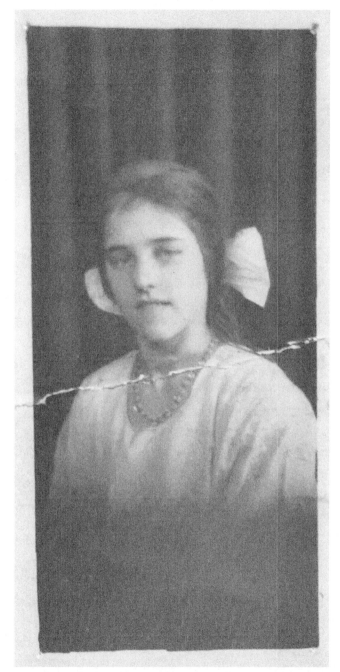

Alice's sister Emma Eckersley (aged 15) Who died August 13th 1947 age 39 leaving behind 5 children

Jealousy

A cup of tea, my old rocking chair and the 'Guardian', my idea of keeping in touch with the world's news in comfort. I do get a bit of a jolt sometimes, even though I do try to keep up with modern thought.

I read about this attractive blonde, who had enjoyed seven years of 'open marriage' and now become suddenly jealous of her husband's friendship with another woman, no wonder she was jealous!

It's the 'open marriage' bit that has me worried. I don't know what it means - could it be that either partner is free to have extra-marital relationships or just that each may enjoy separate and diverse interests whilst keeping to their marriage vows?

She seems to believe people in traditional relationships wouldn't understand her problem; I wanted to reassure her, no one is above jealousy. Her reactions are normal, solving her problem is hers.

Jealously' the word even looks ugly in print, pity it's portrayed by such a lovely colour- green - so many shades matching the various degrees and intensity of the emotion down to the dark green of bitter gall.

There are people incapable of feeling pain because of a malfunction of the nervous system - but to be incapable of jealousy would be equally abnormal.

Jealousy is as much part of the basic human emotions as loving is and we must learn how to deal with both. When we love we try not to hurt the loved one and we know that

giving cause for jealousy is hurting.

These words need to be understood by both partners in any kind of marriage. In the following is my experience of 'Jealousy'.

Many years ago, I had an operation for the removal of a lump in my breast can you imagine my state of mind? I'd even got so far as thinking of my funeral, but do you know what made my heart ache? What caused the feeling of desolation, what thoughts I had to keep to myself? That after my demise my husband would eventually drift into marriage. We were only in our forties, and he was a lively, gregarious person and a solitary existence would have been too cruel to contemplate for him. But I couldn't bear the thought of some other woman in his arms, although I knew what we had had could never be replaced by any other woman. But, oh, the agony of those thoughts that my friend, was unreasoning jealousy.

Needless to say, the lump was benign, my thoughts remained my secret, but I never forgot!

A few years later when my husband and I were still in our early fifties I had to nurse him through a terminal illness.

To nurse without hope, to see the loved one dying, to pretend the inevitable was not happening, then suddenly to be confronted by the truth and reality - by the patient.

Early one morning he held my hand and said, "Love, I know I am dying and I want you to make me a promise - please don't remarry. I love you so and I'll wait for you."

I knew what thoughts he had, they had once been mine - we know dying is a lonely road and one should not have to travel it with heartache as a companion.

Maybe we won't admit the green-eyed monster exists, my friends it does, some may know how to deal with it, but oh, the hard lessons before attaining that knowledge!

Postscript a week later. When I read the article by Anne Hooper in the Guardian, I felt sorry for her, but puzzled by the thought that a marriage counsellor would enter into her type of relationship - 'open marriage' - with such a naive approach!

But I'm elderly, working class and a widow, so maybe I'm old fashioned, but I felt sorry for the girl, and I thought I'd write and comfort her by assuring her, jealousy is a normal emotion, and I was willing to bare a 'raw nerve' in the process then I read the 'Sunday Times' 14.3.82 and do I feel mad!

We have a pile of letters, marvellous stuff, there's a book in it Thames TV want to do a documentary.

That was her husband's statement.

I'm glad I didn't send my letter, I'd have felt as though I'd been exposed to a voyeur - baring a raw nerve, for someone else's profit - but, as I say, I'm old fashioned and my set of principles antiquated, but this kind of gimmick sticks in my gullet.

Jehovah Weeps

Jehovah weeps as his creation is torn asunder in a frenzy of destruction
His words to the prophets misconstrued – and disbelieved!
Man, now takes on his makers role, and wrecks his own kind of vengeance
on fellow man
With disbelief in a 'hereafter' he lives but for today
He lusts for power, hungers for gold, and yearns for domination for mankind

Mother nature despairs to see her fair earth so ravished by this creature man
And knowing the ultimate destruction of her planet
Sees only one consolation, the annihilation of his species

Jetson

The prisoner of industry his shackles now removed by man's
inventiveness
Sees not the freedom so bestowed.
The treadmill of his servitude is stilled No more his feet to pace its steady
rhythm - or -
Mindful of the need to keep in step at long last he is free! Free - for what? To
rust away like his now obsolete machine and dream away the empty days,
redundancy so callously
bestowed
With the tunnel vision of his kind - He yearns - For things familiar - the
rattle of his chains The treadmills clank Steel web of circumstances is
prison's bars!

Love and Marriage

D uring my teenage years life was stark, poverty and ignorance marched together hand in hand, but Mother Nature still held sway; no man or circumstance could prevent her design for the continuity reproduction of mankind!

Along with the majority of my generation I was naïve, my knowledge of sex and human biology was abysmal, but I find it hard to decide whether our ignorance caused as many complications as today's open attitude to and knowledge of sex!

The Workhouse' or a 'shot gun wedding' was the 'Sword of Damocles', which added spice or guilty despair to anyone tasting pre-nuptial sex.

I remember too, when I was young and in love and how wonderful life was sixty-five years ago.

My boyfriend had been to my home and so, according to local tradition, established the fact that we were courting and some day in the distant future we would marry.

The distant future' - that was the problem: he was only a precer, an apprentice cotton spinner, earning a small wage and no prospect of any increment until he inherited 'dead men's mules' in what literally was the distant future'. Probably a minimum of ten years, hence, was daunting, as our relative ages were then 23 years and 19 years.

Love won't wait 10 years at least not the love of young impatient humans, and the inevitable happened - I became pregnant!

No need for a shotgun - the groom was willing, and the bride though apprehensive was of like mind.

What mixed emotions gripped me, the future bride? The longing to share his bed and bear his child-then to be faced with the nightmare of reality - his pittance of a wage which was hardly sufficient to provide for his bare necessities. How would we survive?

This being I carried within my womb both trilled and haunted me - oh, how I wished it wasn't there, but oh how I treasured it! If only well if it had only put off for a few years, its appearance.

Samuel Laycock knew how I felt -

Thart welcum, little bonny brid but the shouldn't a cum just when tha did Times are bad!

That said it all-, but we had a solution! My sweethearts' sisters knew of a 'sure cure' - 'grate one whole nutmeg into a good tot of gin, warm in a saucepan and drink in bed on retiring.

Both my sweetheart and I just thought menstruation would resume - we hadn't a clue what a miscarriage entailed!

Thus, he brought the gin and I used one of my mothers' nutmegs, carried out the instructions and meantime asking my young sister to bring the concoction upstairs.

when I had got into bed, then to wash out the cup thoroughly. We were the only two in the house at the time and after bravely swallowing the foul drink I was soon fast asleep, but all night felt on fire. As soon as my mother came home, the smell of warm gin told its own tale as my sister hadn't rinsed the cup and told mother of the 'medicine' I had taken, she decided not to waken me but to wait 'till the following morning for an explanation. The following morning, I got wearily out of bed and the room spun round, then my mother came into the room and informed me that she knew of the concoction I had swallowed and to what purpose!

Then she really went to town' - 'didn't I realise that no man should ask the woman he loved to risk her life by such means!' - and 'who had given us the recipe for this so-called remedy?'

I had to tell her, and she informed me that 'should I miscarry, she would tell the family doctor the full story'. She thought that anyone who would encourage another to commit such an act should be punished!

When my boyfriend called that evening, she told him that in no uncertain terms what she thought of the whole episode. Needless to say, the cure wasn't effective, my pregnancy didn't terminate and the plans for our wedding went ahead.

We married one Saturday Morning in early November in the local parish Church - my sister-in-law and her boyfriend were witnesses.

We went to live with his widowed mother and an elder sister, and I continued to work for a time during my pregnancy.

The expected delivery date of April 18th came and passed without anyone showing concern - first babies are never on time. Thus, on the 5th May my husbands' family decided I should make an effort, a pram being offered by a local furniture dealer to the parents of the first child born on the following day May 6th the silver Jubilee of the accession of King George and Queen Mary,

That evening I was given a mixture of orange juice and caster oils and the following morning around 4am it became effective and slow labour started.

It was a lovely sunny day, but there was a hot, dry wind when my husband went off to work at 7.15am and his mother prepared to start the usual Monday task - washing day!

She laundered and the clothes dried. I ironed. By mid-day my back ached intensely.

the mid-wife was sent for, and I was put to bed.

I knew my baby would be delivered PV and that the process would be painful, but this was the extent of my knowledge. With every pain I was filled with terror - instead of relaxing I tensed up and at 7pm when my baby was born, I was completely exhausted.

Bathes and dressed in swaddling clothes, my baby was placed in my arms and the midwife went downstairs to get a well-earned cup of tea for both nurse and patient.

I cannot describe the wonder of motherhood as I held my baby. She was the fulfilment of our love, and she was so like him - then tears dropping slowly down my cheeks as other emotions took hold-I felt vulnerable, inadequate and so fearful of our future - what had I done? The only thing my child would have is plenty of love! Would this be enough?

But we were young, and we did have love and hope of a brighter future - someday! Bern By the way we didn't win the pram- my baby was the last one that day!

*Alice and Lambert on holiday in Blackpool in 1950s. Alice sat on Lambert's Knee,
Sister Phylis sat on the right side of Alice*

Alice with daughter Ann (on knee) Sheila and son Gordon 1939

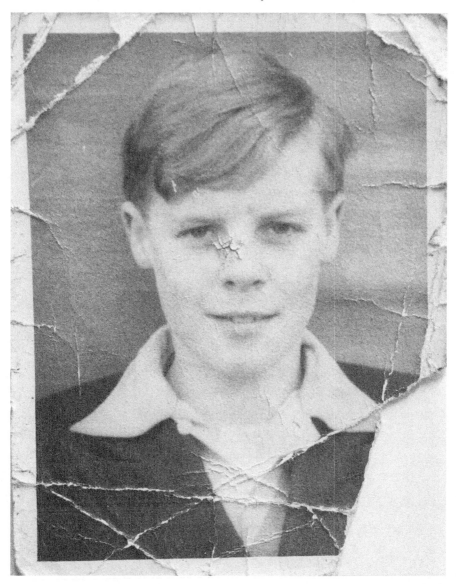

Stanley Alice's youngest child born 1941 (school photo 1954-Nov)

Man's Art

See the canvas in your mind's eye That vast expanse so full of colour
Brown mixed with purple gushing from oil wells Gold from which the world economy is built
Man's greed not Need is painted here and silvery white nuclear reactors and weapons gleaming Amidst the ochre of defoliants
But where is mankind?
No time to paint him, he has too many faces
Besides the canvas his creation
Mankind is Gods!

Morning Assembly

E ach morning after the marking of the attendance registers, every pupil from standard I upwards, assembled in the big room for morning prayers and a service, given by Mr Redfern the headmaster. With a clatter of iron shod clogs on the wooden floor pupils from standards I, II, III, IV left their classrooms to join the senior classes seated in the row of desks, then Mr Redfern mounting the platform greeted the assembly- 'Good Morning Children and with one accord answered-'Good Morning Sir'. The service opened with a hymn, then the 'Lords Prayer", which we sang accompanied on the piano by Mr Redfern; we then seated facing the centre of the room where Mr Redfern now stood to give us a scripture lesson.

He had the ability to capture the interest of all- his telling, the explaining and meaning of the parables and miracles- the gradual build up to Christmas and Easter with the bible stories, the Old Testament with the history of the Jews, the New Testament, gave the children the tenants of Christianity and the Unitarian belief of "The Brotherhood of Man'.

For me this was an ideal start to the day, the lesson given by the son of a Unitarian minister. So many lovely hymns:

'Awake my soul and with the sun'
'Father lead me day by day' 'By cool Siloam's shady rill'
'Hark, hark my soul angelic songs are swelling'

'Eternal father strong to save'
'Hushed was the evening hymn' (one of my favourites)

So many loved hymns of which I have only mentioned a few. So many lovely memories of a happy childhood, a good school and loving home, now the glowing embers in the dying fire of life, which often give warmth in old age.

Now in old age each weekday at 9.45 am, I sit in my rocking chair and listen to Radio 4's Morning Service- if they sing an old familiar hymn 'my day is made', and I join in because there is no one there to hear my wavering voice. I get very annoyed if they forget to say the lord's prayer.

The service ends a few seconds before the 10am radio pips, but I remain seated to reminisce a while.The clatter of iron shod clogs on the wooden floor see the boys and girls of my school days. Three I remember who gave their lives in the second world war.

Side door entrance to the "Big Room" Chowbent School

Infants Department, Chowbent School

Chowbent Chapel

New Moon

When I drew the curtains of my sitting room, as dusk fell, I glimpsed the New Moon peeping above the house tops and I remembered when - many, many years ago another New Moon peeping through the trees in the garden of a T.B. Sanatorium where I was a patient.

I was 17 years old and after surgery in a general hospital for the removal of bovine T.B. glands, I was sent to recuperate at Rufford Hospital near Southport. Rufford Hospital - to me - my 'Shangri-la', My bed along with another 9, each one with a patient suffering from some sort of T.B., on a veranda facing a walled garden with a lilly pond surrounded by a rose garden and majestic trees through which the breeze rustled, and owls made their nests.

This was another world, there was another quality of life I'd never met before - or since and the realisation that there is only today, each moment to be savoured as though sipping from the wine of life.

I see them now in my minds eye fellow patients - did they have the saree optimism as me? I knew I would recover and go home again. I knew my biggest battle had been fought and won by skilled surgeons at Bolton Royal Hospital and what I needed now was TLC and now the highlight of Sanatoria treatment.

I was just like most of girls of my age, had romantic ideas of someday falling in love and marrying - but who would want a former T.B. patient - just like the lepers of biblical times we were 'unclean' even if we didn't have to go round ringing our bell - friends and neighbours all knew.

In the late 20's there was New Moon' being performed in London and the female star was Evelyn Laye a beautiful young woman with a lovely voice, excerpts were heard on the radio and at home we had a 'Masters Voice' horned gramophone on which we played a record of the lovely songs.

This certain day I had been in the recreation room when the music of 'New Moon' came over the ether. I certainly couldn't compete with Evelyn Laye, but I could sing in tune so, I joined in!

"You went away I let you, we broke the tie that binds
I wanted to forget you and leave the past behind
Still the magic of the night I met you, seems to stay forever in my
mind
The sky was blue and high above, the moon was new and so was love,
This eager heart of mine was singing 'lover where can you be?"
-you came at last, love had its day –
That day is past, you've gone away, this aching heart of mine is
saying lover come back to me!
Remembering all the little things you used to say and do - I'm so lonely –
Every road I've walked along I've walked along with you -
No wonder I am lonely!
The sky is blue, the night is cold, the moon is new, but love is old
And whilst I'm waiting here this heart of mine is saying
'Lover Come Back to Me'"

That evening as I was preparing for bed one of my fellow patients Mrs Hayes asked if I would sing the song we'd heard in the recreation room, I forgot the excuse I made for refusing, but not the reason for my refusal.

Sleeping on the balcony above were 2 sisters, 1 whose engagement was broken off by her fiancé when she caught T.B.

Some of my fellow patients had left at home husbands and children and I would I find someone out there to fall in love - with me? Some day would the new moon bring me someone who would love me? I just couldn't remind my fellow patients of the ache of loneliness for many lost love at time when they needed love most - I'm afraid I would have wept!

Please

Grant me a niche at your fireside
At the even of my days
A helping hand, a welcoming smile
To help me on my way
Sometimes a plate at your table
A thought in your evening prayer

Poverty

Poverty is the mantle freely donned by monk or nun
As proof of their humility
Poverty is a shackle made for man - by man
It restricts ambition and inhibits thought
Welded by apathy, his dreams lie in the dust –
To wither in his excrement.

Reflection

An old woman is reflected in my mirror
With lack lustre eyes
Lifeless grey locks above a furrowed brow
Gnarled work worn hands
Arthritic joints and varicose kegs
But oh!

The lovely memories of the past
When my step was light, and my face was fair
And my babies nestled within my arms
These are the thoughts that give warmth
To a cold and of times lonely old age

Alice (age 19) with Niece Joyce Farmworth (age 2)-The colliery in the background, Tyldesley

Remembering Home

13 Garden Place, a small, terraced house in a row of five.

Parents Sarah and John Eckersley and family of 9 children

Its Sunday morning and Mother preparing dinner as she prepared veg ready cooking, lovely mezzo soprano voice accompanied with my father's voice and children joining in. Looking back how fortunate we children were to have such happy home with such loving parents.

the Great Thou Art" "Before Jehovah's awful throne" also carols at Christmas.

Christmas. "Whispering Hope" song of the time.

The last time I saw our Vera. She was sat on their couch and as I sat down with her, she took my hand and said, "Alice sing this with me - "Sing me to sleep" and I did.

> "Sing me to sleep whilst shadows fall
> Let me forget this world & all
> Tired is my heart the day is long
> Wish I would come to eversong
> Sing me to sleep your hand in mine
> Our fingers as in prayer entwined
> Only your voice love let me hear
> Telling again that you are near

Love I am lonely years are so long
I want you only you and your song
Dark is nights shadow days are so long
Leave me no more love sing me to sleep
A true story of my mother"

Retirement

Now the ticking clock is stilled
The alarm no longer shrills
"Awake 'tis time for work"
The hours no longer measure
Sleep, work, sleep, work
Now time divides -sleep-
Followed by endless hours of –
Unused, unpaid, unproductive time!

Rufford 'Shangri La'

~~~~~~~~~~~~~~~

Mae Murray, a twenty-three-year-old, dark haired young woman, was my fellow traveller in the ambulance to Rufford Hospital. She came from Farnworth and was the only child of elderly parents. Her mother, a diabetic, was partially blind.

Rufford at last, through the lodge gates and down the long drive to what was once a former country home of the Hesketh family.

A gracious building with wards that opened out to a walled garden and lily pond. Patients' beds on the veranda facing the garden and a balcony above with more patients' beds.

We entered by what would have formerly been the tradesmen's entrance. The ambulance driver handed over our suitcase to the nurse who answered the doorbell and she escorted us through a small hall, ten the patients dining room and out to the veranda. Two four-bedded wards opened out onto this veranda, and we were taken into the first one.

After taking our T.P.R.'s the nurse took us to the bathroom and after our bath we dressed in our night clothes, then taken to the surgery to be weighed and afterwards examined by Dr Laird, a tall, elegant, white-haired gentleman with a kind, fatherly manner. We then spent the rest of the day in bed and for several weeks I was only allowed up at 2 p.m., then back to bed at 7pm.

The ward we had been admitted to was a most impressive room, high-ceilinged and beautiful fireplace and containing four beds. One door opened on to another four-bed ward and a door on the opposite wall led to the wood-panelled recreation room. The door by which we had entered gave out on to a veranda which had open access to the large rose garden and lily pond, majestic trees through which the breezes rustled, and birds made their nests.

This was another world. Here was another quality of life I'd never met before-or since; the realisation that there was only today, each moment to be savoured as though sipping from the wine of life, each new day a gift!

I see them now in my mind's eye, fellow patients - did they have the same optimism as me? I knew I would recover and go home again; I knew my biggest battle had been fought and won by the surgeon at Bolton Royal Infirmary. What I now needed was rest, T.L.C. and nourishment (the highlight of sanatoria treatment).

Once ambulant, each patient was given a small domestic task to perform after the 10a.m. rest period. Polishing the brass door handles, polishing the cutlery, wet dusting locker tops, etc. and I was given the job of caring for the vases of flowers, changing the water, etc. There were two ward maids, stepsisters - Violet and I forget the name of the other one.

There were four nurses, one probationer, one night nurse, one sister and one matron - a rather small staff for the number of patients, but one must remember most patients made their own beds and there were very few dressings and artificial pneumothorax treatment was on Monday morning only.

I remember Mary Magdeline Hardman, a nineteen-year-old nurse who had been nursing in a private nursing home. She was the only child of elderly parents, and she was engaged to a

farmer, a tanned, well-built, well-dressed young man. She was beautiful with a lovely smile that showed teeth like pearls. What puzzled me was her appearance on admission. She was bonny and her limbs were 'well covered'. unlike the usual emaciated looking patients on admission.

Three weeks later she was dead - from 'galloping consumption'. Elsie, a pretty thirteen-year-old, golden red curly hair, blue eyes and fair complexion, with the pink cheeks, cherry lips and bright eyes consumption usually bestowed on its victims. She had won a scholarship to a grammar school.

Her mother was dead, and her father had re-married, and one could deduce from her conversation the hurt she felt at the replacing of her mother by his new wife. Her most frequent visitor was her sister, a well-dressed young woman in her mid-twenties. Her father also visited.

Elsie's ward had to be decorated, so her bed was transferred to the recreation room meanwhile. The following Sunday morning I called in to see her. Painfully and laboured, she told me of the pain in her chest. A few hours later she haemorrhaged and died-.

In this place death was just part of the dream. Any grief felt by the rest of the patients was hidden, no tears shed for the loss of a friend, only a quiet acceptance of the inevitable.

Two little girls in adjoining beds near mine, after I'd been moved from the ward to the veranda Mary, a lovely, dark-haired chatterbox of 7 years with the deadly bloom already apparent on her features, had a father suffering from the disease.

Mona Atherton, a quiet little five-year-old who came from Squires Lane, Tyldesley. She had had pneumonia, which had left fluid on her lungs. In later years I heard she had died at the age of fifteen. Somehow, I feel sure she would have recovered and survived had she been left home. I met her family, and they were loving and caring and their home comfortable.

I remember two patients, sisters who were in the ward with the balcony above our veranda; they were both very attractive with light brown curly hair, they had been typists and the younger one had been engaged. Alas, she had been jilted because of her TB. Neither looked seriously ill, but one needed hope and something to live for to fight TB. Rejection by anyone to a TB patient would only destroy the will to live. Heartache and TB are certainly not compatible.

I only remember two nurses' names: Staff Nurse Hesketh and probationer Goodacre, but I can still visualize the others – the big, plump night nurse who brought the 6 a.m. cup of tea (like treacle), the dark-haired Welsh nurse, always dressed in the height of fashion on her day off, which she spent in Southport. Back to reality, an overcrowded insanitary terraced house, which somehow was a real home, with a loving, caring family.

I would be part of the living world once more; work would no longer be a daily painful trudge. I had healthy limbs; walking was a pleasure.

I had an appetite for life as well as food. this being once a tom boy, then an invalid, was now back home with a zest for life.

Back to the world which nature said I now belonged to, the teenage world of the emotional seesaw of happiness, despair, love, hate, cowardice and courage.

At the age when Mother Nature in her determination to continue procreation gives the frogs the guises of handsome princes, and where, in spite of overwork, malnutrition and poverty, procreation in the guise of love continued.

Mae Murray, the patient admitted with me, died at the age of twenty-eight.

I look at the snapshots taken now 60 years ago and wonder at the life span of my friends shown there:

Phyllis Clayton from Seaforth had lost a nineteen-year-old brother from consumption and Phyllis had the cough and tell-tale rosy cheeks with augured ill.

Several of the patients had served long periods in other TB Sanatoria; they would be discharged, go back home to the same conditions which had probably been the cause of their illness in the first place-over-crowding, malnutrition and insanitary living conditions. I think poverty and ignorance were to blame for most cases of TB. Matron was fair with pale red hair and always dressed in lovely pastel-coloured cotton uniforms. Sister in the usual navy dress and white apron (she had nursed in the 1914-18 war).

Whilst a patient I had two teeth extracted by Dr Laird in the little theatre.

I sat on a small stool whilst my head rested on the operating table. After a local anaesthetic Dr Laird began the first extraction. His grip on the instrument he used wasn't very good and half-way through the procedure he had to renew his hold.

Eventually the tooth was extracted, and I thought the effort worth the pain as the toothache had caused me several nights' loss of sleep. A couple of weeks later the second tooth was extracted by the same method and sister seemed to admire my fortitude in enduring a repeat of the first extraction.

Rufford Old Hall, Rufford, West Lancashire

Alice went to convalesce in Rufford

Rufford 1932 (pulmonary hospital). Alice and other patients (Alice front centre)

Alice, and other girls (patients Agnes and Hester) playing croquet in Rufford Gardens 1932

Sarah and Son

There is no life of a man faithfully recorded. Bit is a heroic poem of its sort rhymed or unrhymed - Thomas Carlyle.

Sarah had slept fitfully and the whole panorama of her married life seemed to flit between dreams and consciousness. She must get up as soon as the alarm sounded at 7 a.m., but meantime her memory had begun a re-run of the scenario started twenty-two years ago, and in which today's forthcoming event would be the climax.

She remembered how, at the beginning of it all her heart had felt.

like lead-she prayed she was mistaken, she already had seven children and her husband, John, was a "poor provider", his job as a haulage hand in a local colliery was poorly paid.

To help support the family Sarah 'took in washing', and several days a week spent many weary hours over steaming tubs of hot soapy water rubbing and scrubbing bundles of other families' soiled clothing.

And now, she was sure she was pregnant again.

In her past pregnancies she'd always felt dispirited in the first three months, feverishly willing her body to produce evidence to the contrary. But in the past, once the vital third month was over, and the sign's showed pregnancy was a certainty the nature of mother took possession of her being and she was always filled with a warmth and a welcome that nothing and no-one could diminish.

Not this time though, there was no joy in this pregnancy. She'd had enough of struggling to make ends meet' and could find no welcome for this 'being' within her. It had no right, no right, to come where it wasn't wanted - It wouldn't get a Samuel Laycock's welcome -

"Tha'rt welcome little bonny brid
But the shouldn'cum just when tha did,
Times are bad!"

It had no right to stay where it wasn't wanted - no right to come and add to her burden, she was so tired, so weary of this miserable existence - that's all it was a miserable existence.

When she booked old Sarah Jimpy, the local midwife, for the confinement, her spirits weren't even raised when the old dame repeated her usual compliment to Sarah - "Tha'll mak a sweet owd woman Sarah, Tha alus lets Nature tek her own sweet way."

The old woman knew Sarah, had never taken any noxious potions or attempted any other means to procure abortion, but little did she know how grimly Sarah believed that solution would have been kinder to the unborn child.

The birth was straight forward, and Sarah was delivered a son. After bathing the baby Old Sarah went forward to place him in his mother's arms. The midwife couldn't believe her eyes: Sarah had refused to take the child and she motioned the midwife to lay him on the bed away from her. She paid the old woman her five shillings midwifery fee and the old woman went on her way, after promising to come the following morning to continue her duties, which would entail for the next ten days bathing the baby and routine attention to his mother.

The baby was very quiet; true it yelled enough on its entrance into the world, but now, not a murmur - was there something wrong with it, she wondered? Well, she just wasn't interested. It had no right, no right, to be here - but it was here, and she was - It's mother some mother! Why, she wasn't worthy of the name.

In a frenzy Sarah turned, picked up the child and cradled him close to her breast, berating herself as she rocked him gently to and fro. What a welcome, what a beginning to a new life, and suddenly the love she had tried to deny him welled up in her being and somehow, she felt as if he claimed a special place in her heart.

When the rest of the family came into the bedroom to view the newcomer, he was displayed with all the love and pride that had been bestowed on the rest of his sisters and brothers on their arrival.

Sarah's life continued as before and the laundering and drudgery seemed never ending, but somehow the love she bore her family made it all seem worthwhile and, in the evenings, before she put the children to bed, always managed to tell a fairy story or sing the songs she'd learned in her childhood and youth.

Two and a half years later when Sarah was forty-four years old, she gave birth to a daughter and Sarah was sure there would be no more pregnancies; but she was mistaken and when she was forty-seven became pregnant for the last time. This time she was desperately ill. Over Christmas she had 'flu, which by New Year's Eve had developed into pneumonia and

at the height of the crisis was delivered of a daughter, three months premature and approximately one and a half pounds in weight.

She never saw the child, but later on had been told how it had been wrapped in cotton wool and placed in a grocer's wicker order basket, which was put on the steel fender on one side of the living room fireplace and there the child survived for fifteen hours. No attempt was made to fight for this feeble life - what was the use? The mother was dying, and God only knew what was to become of the other ones!

She never even knew where it had been buried. It had been placed in a cardboard shoe box and taken to the cemetery by the newly qualified midwife (who had been in attendance at the birth) and Sarah's daughter-in-law, Mary.

The wee corpse was then handed over to the cemetery official who would arrange to have it place in any available open grave, alongside the coffin of any person buried that day, which was the custom at the time for any child under 48 hours of life.

The wife of a local colliery owner was ill at the same time and although she had the best care and attention money could buy, both she and her unborn child died.

Sarah remembered this, comparing the attention she had received - caring neighbours popping in with lemon drink, sago gruel, beef tea, anything to keep aflame that dying spark of life. Her special friend, also named Sarah, who had been Godmother to her last three children and who by her presence and help encouraged Sarah in her fight for life.

Once again, she recalled how she had burned with fever, and in her delirium watched the flickering candle flame on the mantlepiece perform a grotesque ballet with the dancing shadows cast by the iron of the bed rails. The burning coals in the grate, the hiss of the gas then the subsequent jet of flame and she seemed to take her place amid the burning coals; the unquenchable thirst, the racking cough, the pain, all remembered with such clarity as though it had happened only yesterday.

The cooling words of prayer which had been uttered by the trim figure who had knelt at her bedside - Miss Faywell - who had helped run the Mission Hall with Miss Rawlinson, daughter of the Mission's founder.

Miss Faywell in her high-necked, long-sleeved navy dress with the little touches of cream lace peeping out above the high neckline and around the sleeve cuffs. The shallow navy hat perched on her head with a neat bun in full support and the little tendrils of hair which escaped the restrictions of hair pins, and the face beneath, love, compassion and, as she'd prayed for Sarah's life, the earnest pleading in her voice.

The God to whom she had prayed was a God of love and compassion and Sarah had always believed this gentle creature's daily prayers had given her strength in her fight for life.

She remembered also, how, during her convalescence her little 'unwanted bundle' had sat on the edge of her bed telling her of the wonderful gifts he was going to 'buy' her.

The child had seen a funeral where, for the first time, he had
seen a motor-hearse used. In their neighbourhood the usual custom was that the coffin was conveyed to the cemetery on the shoulders of male relatives or friends, or in the case of the more affluent, a horse-drawn hearse was used.

Seeing the glass and ebony case of the new-style motor-hearse. The lovely wreaths and the polished wooden coffin with the brass handles, had created such an impression on the child's mind. He had never seen such beauty, such perfection and - such a conveyance.

He knew the coffin had contained a dead person and in facet he had known the man. He had also heard the word dying associated with his mother and her illness, and as he'd sat on her bed, he regaled her with stories of the lovely gifts he would love to buy her - a lovely, polished coffin with gold handles, beautiful wreaths of flowers and, most important of all, the lovely glass, motor-driven carriage to "take her in".

That this was the ultimate in gifts had made Sarah smile whilst realizing the poignancy of the situation to get well, and so, not to destroy her child's dreams of a beautiful funeral for his mother for it would only have been a dream - she would have got the usual conveyance to the cemetery: on the shoulders of male relatives and friends.

Life went on and when this son was fourteen years old, he went to work down the mine on the haulage.

Sarah now had five children working and one at school; but John, her husband, was now an invalid with an income of nine shillings weekly, half sick benefit, because he had been off work over six months, after which period, payment was halved. This was the early thirties, and all the children's wages together didn't make a man's wage, but one thing she was determined on - no more bundles of other folk's washing. From now on, just her own family's washing, and the life of an ordinary housewife, cleaning, cooking, and baking.

The next memory was one of seven years later, only three children now remained at home; the others had married. John was still in receipt of his nine shillings sick pay which was just eight pence short of the rent of their new council house. It was her youngest son's twenty-first birthday and Sarah remembered with pride that day, how he had announced, "you'll have no more money worries, mother, from now on I'll be on full pay and will get a man's wage." His unopened pay envelope handed over, she gave him pocket money and paid the weekly payments on his bike on which he travelled to work.

She was so proud of him, his fair hair, clear skin and lovely teeth, so honest, so hardworking and so loved - he who had been so unwanted at birth. But over the years Sarah had tried to drown the feeling of guilt in a sea of love.

Sarah never went to the second house at the cinema. In fact, she seldom went to the cinema at all those days, preferring to listen to the wireless until twenty minutes to ten, then slipping her shawl on and going down for a gill of stout to bring home to take with her supper.

Her son had seen a film, "Maytime", in which there was some good singing and he'd pleaded with his parents to go and see it.

He was on the night shift and his sister would see to his supper, so his mother and father could go to the second house, and they would not need to rush back.

The film was everything he'd said it was, the music and the singing a real treat, but on their way home there seemed to be flashes of light on Bolton Road.

When they got home, the house was full. All her sons and daughters were there, all except one, the one who was left to cook her son's supper. What was wrong? Bill - her Bill had been

killed and her daughter, Alice, had gone to identify him.

It had all been a horrible nightmare. If only she'd been home to give him his supper. If only, if only! Was this her punishment for denying him at birth? Oh no, she'd made up for all that. In fact, the special place he'd held in her heart was her way of compensating.

She prayed it was all a dream and would be gone by morning, but morning came, and reality was a nightmare. No-one could comfort her. In fact, the rest of the family seemed as distraught as she: they'd all loved him so and they all knew how special he was to her and to them too.

The inquest and funeral had all been a bad, vague, happening in which Sarah had the sensation of only being an onlooker - it wasn't real you know - she'd be glad when she awoke.

There'd been an article in the local evening paper and the story of how proud he'd been when he could help remove financial cares from his mother's shoulders. Another article too - misadventures - a learner driver had been driving the trolley bus which had caught his bicycle's back wheel as he entered High Street on his way to Tyldesley Road.

The water from his pit can showed the impact and speed of the bus was such that he and his bike had been carried nearly two hundred yards.

Sarah hardly comprehended any of this at the time. Her son, Jack, had got a solicitor to act on his parent's behalf so he had represented them at the inquest. The only other person there, the daughter who had last seen Bill alive, then later identified him, and could not repeat any of the proceedings to her parents, the wound was too new and too painful.

The alarm sounded, Sarah got up, washed, dressed, then prepared breakfast for John and herself. They'd both have to be ready for ten o'clock. The solicitor was coming to pick them up to take them to Liverpool to see the barrister who was to represent them in their claim for damages.

Solicitor - hm - a small plumpish man, his dark hair slick and oily - and his manner matched. Sarah couldn't think why her son had got this man to represent them, she'd trust him as far as she could throw him. Jack had said he was a pillar of the local chapel, well, she'd never seen woodworm, but she could imagine what kind of a face it would have - slick and oily.

He arrived on time - "we must be punctual. Mr. B. doesn't like to be kept waiting - well, actually it isn't done, he's a very important K.C. and he belongs to the same nonconformist religion as myself - not the same chapel you understand, you see he doesn't live in Lancashire, although he has chambers in Liverpool", thus he prattled on as he drove them in his car to Liverpool and this eminent personage.

All the way the words "Blood money, blood money, blood money", were running through Sarah's mind - My God, that's what she was going for blood money - blood money. The money would be tainted, tainted by the blood of that best beloved child - this was too high a price to pay for money - what would she do? - tell this little popinjay to turn back? - but if she did, her little love had died and there was no bringing him back, and he had worked and strived for security for his mother, now, this was his latest tribute.

They eventually arrived at the great man's chambers and were shown in by one of his juniors. The great man, due to appear in court that morning, was in his wig and gown and the sense of his own importance seemed to permeate the room.

Sarah felt sickened by the solicitor's craw deferential manner to the K.C., and felt that, by having this creature escort them here, gave John and her a sense of inferiority, as though contact with him of any kind had demeaned them and their son.

There was no look of sympathy or compassion in the granite of the K.C.'s face and his voice when he spoke was ponderous and cold - Sarah couldn't believe her ears - "the Company have made you an offer - this is it - my advice is - accept - if it went to court you could end up losing your case."

The man was mad! It was almost as though he was charging her son and putting all the blame for the accident upon him! John took hold of her and looked into her eyes. "Agree to anything. Let's get out of this pollution", his eyes seemed to say.

They were on their way home again in the solicitor's car and he was praising his eminent colleague and congratulating them on the award. "I would be quite willing to invest the money for you when you receive it."

Alarm bells rang in Sarah's brain. She had just witnessed justice in action, and she was damn sure none of its representatives were being allowed to juggle with her son's blood money. Once again, she was overwhelmed with a terrible sense of guilt - the money - what could she do with it. She felt like Judas with his thirty pieces of silver. What was more she'd left that place and had never uttered a word in her son's defence. She felt sick at heart and so weary.

It was weeks later when John and Sarah received a letter from the Inland Revenue demanding tax due from a large sum of money, which they had received in damages following the death of their son money they hadn't received a red cent. Sarah replied immediately also stating that the present financial circumstances - nine shillings sick pay weekly to keep John and herself. The only remaining son at home was now supporting them, He was now working on a coal-cutting machine and getting a reasonable wage. Sarah also went to see the solicitor and threatened him with legal action if

85

the money was not forthcoming. She had never given him permission to handle it and it was his duty to hand it over when it was eventually settled.

But whenever she thought of spoke about the money there was always this feeling of distress, and she could never imagine it in the possession of herself of John. They were managing alright now - Alf was a good son and they had no immediate financial worries and nothing and no-one could ease the ache of her heart - nothing would ever be the same again.

It was Christmas Eve. Sarah had baked the pies and cakes which tradition always demanded, but the carols which she had always sung as she prepared for the festivities were absent. In the distance a brass band was playing "Silent Night" and suddenly there was a loud knock on the front door.

Sarah was amazed to see a stranger at the door, a well-dressed young woman and in the roadway a car with the engine running.

The young woman thrust a pile of notes into Sarah's hands with "Your money - it's all there", turned on her heels and ran back to the car, the driver, and they were away!

It was all there, every penny, this gift from her son with the Blessing of Love of Christmas no longer thirty pieces of silver.

Alice's brother Stanley William "Bill" Eckersley who was killed going to work on his bike in 1938

Stanley "Bill" and friend Robert Minshell on holiday (Bill on the bottom step)

Stanley "Bill's" Mother and Father Sarah and John George Eckersley

Stringers Corner Shop

This is not a discourse on the merits or demerits of the present day super-market with their modern shopping facilities as against the old fashioned "corner shop". It's just a closing of the eyes and remembering.

Swan Song

The snores, the coughs, the moans, the sighs
Tis the music of the night
No more good tunes from these old fiddles
The bow strings breaking on their fragile instruments of life!
The only variation on the melody is the call of "nurse"
A patter of feet, a few whispered words
Then once again, the chorus!

The Dreamer Wakes

In overcrowded bedrooms
On overburdened beds we slept
Bodies slotted in like badly fitting jigsaw pieces
Sweaty humanity we dreamt of the bright future –
When machines would take on drudgery
Of drab repetitive labour - then –
We'd be free to enjoy life
Each moment to be treasured
As we take our feet off the treadmill of industry
But today we dreamers are awake
The dream, now reality is a bloody nightmare
Humanity is redundant
Educated for work not leisure
Time hangs around our necks
Like an albatross!
The water snake of death
The price of freedom and our release from bondage

The Geriatric

The laughter lines of youth, now the wrinkles of old age
Failing sight, unsteady gait
Yester years memories clearer than to-days
Are the years exceeding three score and ten a blessing?
Or an unwanted bonus!
When the frailties of age become apparent-
Breaking joints, vague aches and pains
The long weary night's yearning
For the dawn of another bloody day

The Lord's Prayer

Our father which art in heaven
Hallowed be they name
Thy kingdom come, thy will be done
On earth as it is in heaven
Give us this day our daily bread
And forgive us our trespasses
As we forgive those who trespass against us
Lead us not into temptation
But deliver us from evil
For thine is the kingdom
The power and the glory
For ever and ever amen

The Mission Hall

A place now demolished, The Mission Hall in Alma Street, stands out in my memories of childhood; it was founded in the mid nineteenth century by one James Rawlinson and, at the time of which I write was run by his daughter and her friend, Miss Faywell who lived in the adjoining premises.

A painting of the place by a local artist, Clarice Pomfret, was seen by my son Stanley and knowing of the affection I had, and the pleasant memories the place held for me, took me in his car to view it immediately I bought it, alas one important feature was missing that wonderful picture of heaven and hell which had stood in the ground floor window.

Ah, this little mission hall a safe harbour, a place where sinners could be put back on the straight and narrow path. Why, they even had that picture to prove it! And to show how it was done.

That picture, the times I've stood gazing at it whilst I've waited for the doors to open for the Band of Hope meeting or the Sunday School class.

'Heaven and Hell' or, to be more precise a colourful picture showing the 2 routes there.

Hell, the wide downward path crowded by men or women in quate Victorian costume, having a wail of a time drinking, dancing, and smoking, I think sins went in that order, drink, not religion being the opiate of the people, that, was number one.

Dancing, the number 2 sin, this is a temptation of the devil? Somehow, as a child I couldn't fathom this one out - didn't one dance for joy? Admitted one didn't see pictures of angels dancing, but fairies did!

Smoking, number 3, why this? They didn't know then of the health hazard or were they warning me off those cig stumps (dockers) the schoolboys picked out of the gutters and which I could be dared to puff!

Ah, the smiles on the faces of the sinners on their wayward, downward, progress, aren't they aware what awaits at the end of the road? See, there at the bottom of the picture, hell with all those poor lost souls condemned to eternal damnation and burning.

Somehow, I don't have a clear picture of this, I guess I wasn't interested in their final punishment, or else, didn't feel any enthusiasm at the thought of such suffering, so, my interest was in their "sin", my father smoked a pipe, somehow this didn't register as a sin in my mind.

Drink, strong drink, now even I, knew this was a sin, we were told often enough at the Band of Hope meetings, and didn't I pray fervently "please Heavenly Father, don't send my Mother to hell when she dies, she's the world's best Mother, doesn't she take washing into help feed us? - and we love her so much - she only goes to the Mick McCabe's outdoor department to get a gill of stout in a jug to drink at suppertime, that's all and you know, it does her good if you really are Our Father please listen to my prayer!"

I was a child with a child's reasoning, surely, he couldn't eternally damn my mother for slipping on her shawl, hiding her jug under it's folds and slipping out to 'Micks' at ten to ten each evening, if He did, He couldn't be much of a father.

Heaven - ah - the straight and narrow path which went upwards and the people on that path who had faces to match – straight and narrow.

Grass, trees, birds and flowers, well dressed people, all on their leisurely way to the land of milk and honey, funny, I never seem to be interested in that path, it looked so boring even with the colourful background, it always registered as black and white, it seemed so lacking in the rich tapestry of the other path; but then the rewards were great, no hunger, no thirst, no sorrow or pain there, but what if there's no one there that you know or care for???

Miss Rawlinson a well-spoken woman but lacking that nameless something could it be love or was it because her voice was stronger and louder, also she didn't smile as often as Miss Faywell. The yearly anniversary services in which my sister Vera and I took part, wearing for 2 or 3 years the same dresses, laundered by my mother, they were white embroidered voil and we had sashes of electric blue, 2 inches wide satin ribbon, threaded through at the waist, a white cotton underskirt, white socks and black patent leather shoes completed our ensemble.

We sat on a platform in front of the congregation and whilst it was a real effort for me to keep still for a couple of hours, I was always enthralled by one of the preachers who played a flat stringed instrument which sounded like a harp, whilst he preached he would only be a lay preacher, they had no paid clergy, but boy, I bet he'd draw the crowds today.

The Question

Natures blueprint misconceived
Forsaken by Adam
Rejected by Eve
Fought over by contentious mankind
To be – or not to be?
That is the question!
To condemn to an existence of undefined worth – unloved
Or
Returned to the bosom of Mother Earth – unmourned

The Workhouse

n apt name for a place so dreaded by the ordinary working men and women. To end one's days in the "workhouse" was the nightmare which haunted the thoughts of so many.

Through the gates entered the sick, the old, the orphans and the inadequate to be fed, clothed, and sheltered.

The work of the establishment was done mainly by the inmates and domestic work on the hospital wards and inmate's quarters, the laundry, and the kitchen.

At the porter's lodge overnight accommodation was provided for vagrants. They were given food, a bath, and a bed for the night. For this they were expected to do some menial job such as chopping firewood etc,

It was the last refuge of the young woman expecting an illegitimate child, they would be parted, the child to the nursery the mother to the female section where she would be allotted work in one of the various departments.

The sons of aged or sick parents were expected to contribute to their maintenance if only a few shillings weekly.

A Socialist Government took away the stigma of the 'workhouse' and the geriatric hospital modernised the buildings which became slowly but surely a place where the elderly retained their dignity.

Slowly the high sided cot beds were done away with, instead of closing off the ward by putting a screen across the doorway during a bed- pan round each bed had its own curtains for screening off, giving privacy whilst toileting.

Then patients were given pocket money to buy sweets, toiletries etc from the W.V.S trolley, later a dress allowance was given, and patients had their own clothing.

Chiropody and hairdressing were available, day rooms were introduced along with physiotherapy and occupational therapy. Leagues of Hospital Friends collected funds and bought hairdressing equipment, a coach with facilities for wheelchairs and patients. Whilst no one likes to leave their home in their final years, one no longer was haunted by the thought of the 'Workhouse' - well I wasn't?

Mrs Thatcher has changed all that our geriatric hospital "Atherleigh", the old workhouse is almost empty of patients, it's to close finally this year.

There's a lot of 'pie in the sky' under discussion, meanwhile we have mushroom growths of "homes for the elderly" no physio, no occupational therapy, no league of friends, just an easy chair and a telly to boggle the mind - but like the good old workhouse, of the old and sick will be given a bed and food, as for me at 75 years food for thought.

Third World

Who stole my child?
Brother in your nightmare you have bread
Crumbs from your table would make sweet dreams of mine
In this third world not, only hope has gone-
My stake in the future died at my shrivelled breast
No milk, no sustenance there
His dream, his nightmare gone
As will go mine if you ignore
My feeble cries – in death!

Time

What is "time"? It has no coinage
Yet all must spend its currency
The dreamer in reverie, the labourer in toil
The schoolboy begrudgingly in learning and
The lover in ecstasy or pain - so fly the years!
Then all too soon "old age" the coffer almost bare
Time only for reflection!
Regrets, mistakes, dreams unfulfilled, all in the past
Now spending time as though from a miser hoard
Praying for strength enough and courage
To face the spending of one's final days with dignity

To Andrew

Douce not the light that burns within thy breast
With the bitter flow of self-denigration
Life is for living, loving and creating
Away with the past, start anew
Make the most of the gift's life gave to you!

Treasured Possessions

❧⟨◦⟩❧

After over three-fifths of a century I must confess to an accumulation of treasures and they fall into various categories practical, beautiful, or, of just sentimental value, none, I must admit, of any real pecuniary worth.

The most treasured and important my family of course! but I won't bore my readers with descriptions of its members, I happen to love everyone, warts, and all, (actually, they are all perfect!!!)

Instead, I'll write about one of my practical treasures, what shall it be? My wireless!

I'd be so lonely without it, just the touch of a switch and I have a companion, interesting or entertaining me in a variety of subjects; a change of mood and I can change to another station or play around with the dials 'til some sounds strikes a chord of response.

Or shall I tell of my electric blanket, my friend of the dark, cold, wintry nights?

Ah! The luxury of a warm bed on such nights; no cringing as one slips into bed between ice cold sheets, instead, engulfed in a sea of warmth - sheer bliss!

My choice is neither of these, it is my Service washing machine. There it stands, in pride of place in my kitchen, my big, beautiful monument of man's regard for women, who, have laundered his shirts and washed his sweaty socks over the years.

You may wonder why I favour this, but then you have hardly had my experience of washing in the old-fashioned way. To get out the tubs, rubbing board and posser, put a few drops of oil on the 'jumbo' mangle, fill the boiler with water, stoke the coal fire underneath and let the battle commence!"

The water heated, get the "ladling can" and transfer some into the tubs and we are now on our way.

Make sure the water isn't too hot for our hands and then we soap and rub each garment via the board, rubbing the skin off our knuckles as well as the dirt from the clothes.

The procedures we followed, rubbing, scrubbing, possing and mangling. The pain and weariness at the end of a days washing, the aching back from bending over the tubs, the aching arms, and shoulders from scrubbing, possing and mangling, but the pride. and joy is seeing the 'whiter than whites', and the dazzling coloureds drying on the clothesline, and one is as thrilled as a Turner or Constable at the completion of a work of art.

Now, with my friend the 'Service' washer their remains the thrill of the laundress with lines of clean linen and all this without the soul-destroying labour of yore, all is now accomplished with minimum effort.

Do you see why I place so much value on it and why I'm glad I won't be around when earth's energy is running out? Just imagine it'll be back to the tubs, rubbing board, posser and - mangle, but I'll have gone!

If I'm allowed in heaven, it'll be just my luck to be put in the laundry, helping to wash all those white gowns, but I won't mind as long as they have a duplicate of my lovely "Service" washing machine, and I'm sure there'll be no energy crisis "there".

Now all you female sinners, listen to me about the stoking up the fires in "the Other Place", that job is reserved for the men; you don't get off quite so easy, for you, it's back to washing all those mucky, sweaty clothes the men wear but no washing - machines all done in the old-fashioned way. The Tubs, the rubbing board, posser, and jumbo mangle -all without the aid of detergents, as a real punishment there may be no soap! That ought to deter your sinning; get back to the "Straight and Narrow", and you may spend eternity with Alice and her "Service" machine.

P.S. For adults only.

Alas, that's not the end of the story, for some fluke we've got a female Prime Minister and she's made such a bloody mess of the nations economy I can no longer afford the electricity which powers my beautiful washing machine, so now I'm back to square 1- using what I kept as museum pieces - my tub, rubbing board, scrubbing brush and posser! I still can't believe it imagine a woman doing as much for

"Women's Lib", as the law lords have done for Ken Livingston
and London Transport! -
? Put more female candidates up for parliament - she's certainly
put the mockers on that!!

Unemployment – Ode to Thatcher

Who stole my dream and left a nightmare in its place?
No joust in chain mail sporting my lady's favour dreamt I
No fantasy of yore did I desire
My dream was of the present –
Of labour for these hands with just reward for effort
With head held high, knowing that the bitter fruit of charity
My dream is gone, the nightmare is reality
With no awakening from its bonds.

Women in Industry

As a schoolgirl, whenever I thought about my future, I knew that I would have to work in industry, although I longed to use my talent and love for 'arithmetic'.

This would have meant an office job, but these positions were few and far between and open to those with a commercial education. I put dreams to one side and gave my mind to an honest day's work to anyone who employed me. An honest or fair days work for? days' pay-starvation wages monthly!!!

Women were such a plentiful source of cheap labour, I do not remember any single working woman who had a home of her own, they lived either with relatives or friends. None of them had their own ' hearthstones.

So many women had lost prospective husbands in the First World War, so many young men killed, so many women denied marriage and motherhood, so many women condemned to live a hand to mouth' existence for the rest of their working lives with stark reality of the 'Workhouse' in old age.

It's a pity Lowry never portrayed the ugly features of poverty, the 'knock knees', bowlegs, stunted growth, gaunt features and lack lustre eyes!

He painted industry as the background and the limit of our horizon, the 'be all' and 'end all of our existence - we had to earn the cash to buy the food which would provide the energy to work to earn the cash - ad infinitum.

When I worked at Carr and Nichols nut and bolt manufacturers at the age of fourteen, I often saw two sisters who lived in Bolton Rd. nearby; both had badly deformed legs, rickets as children! The elder one was so knocked - kneed that her knees crossed as she walked, but she managed to work in the New Rd Cotton Mill.

The other sister was terribly bow-legged and didn't go out to work. Both sisters were pretty, fair skinned and curly haired and very neat in appearance. Knock - Knees and bow-legs' were not an unusual sight around this time but theirs were gross deformities.

There is no freedom in being a slave to a machine where the rewards are insufficient to keep the body fuelled for the task, when the wages are insufficient for one's basic needs this is the cause of malnutrition, underlying factor of many diseases- rickets, T. B., premature death the hidden price of the 2 good old days!

Alice age 15 (on the right) and friends Edna Battersby and Nellie Sloane at Carr and Nichols Smithy-Approx 1930 (wearing clogs)

Alice-photo taken approx 1932 at Carr and Nichols works outing to Blackpool

Work

Easter 1929 I left school on Thursday with a sad heart and the following Tuesday commenced work in the ring spinning department at Howebridge Mills (No2 mill)

Always conscious of poverty, yet at home and school there was a feeling of security, at home there was love, at school there was learning, and I had a hunger for both!

That Tuesday, I felt like a babe now of birth- thrust from the warmth of the womb into the cold unknown; from now on I must work to provide for my means of sustenance by contributing to the family purse.

My father was an invalid, and, in those days, there was no welfare State only the workhouse the family income was from two older sisters and a brother working in the mule spinning department, on very low wages and a brother working on the haulage in the mine- our wages were pulled in, mother held the purse.

As a learner my first week's wage was 3/11 (approx. 20p) for five and a half days working week, but the following week I was promoted to scavenger, not because I could do the job, but to make up complement needed for a set number of frames so then my wage was 13/- weekly- a fantastic wage for a 14 yr. old! However, this did not last long- the ring frames were stopped, lack of orders, so I was given work in the card room leaning rusting carding machines which had not been in use for months.

These machines were large and there were several covering a large area and I was alone cleaning these machines with emery paper, oil, and waste cotton.

It was a lonely job for a gregarious child, but I worked with a will realising the value of the money earned.

A couple of weeks of this then the whole mill came to a standstill, so I along with the workers in the other departments became unemployed.

There was no 'dole' (unemployment pay) for me as one did not contribute to the National Insurance Fund until the age of 16 yrs. (I got a job in the nut and bolt industry.)

I'll never forget that short period in the cotton mill- working all day under electric lighting- the noise- the rattle of the rings and the whirring of the bobbins- deafening.

Breathing in cotton fibres, the sour smell of raw cotton- the sickly smell of hot machine oil- I was trapped like a bird in a cage at the age of 14yrs- the long hours of daylight and my freedom sold for a pittance.

My elder sister Emma worked as a half- timer at the age of 13yrs- working in the morning going to school in the afternoon then alternate the following week. Often the morning workers fell asleep at their desk sin the afternoon!

By the way my late husband was a cotton spinner where the custom was working as a 'pieces' for a pittance and waiting for promotion via- 'dead men's mules'.

Yours

Alice Cook DoB 21/1/1915

Lancashire Labour Laws

N o Mention is made of the poor sods who worked in the mill, they were regarded as sub-human.

In the Highland clearances the Scottish lairds turfed their clansman off the land when they realised sheep were more profitable occupants.

The sheep in Lancashire were even more profitable, they worked in the mills. No need to eat their fleece, the owners managed to fleece them without laying hands on them - ah man, the greediest and most devious of animals.

LANCASHIRE LABOUR LAWS
1852

The following "Rules and Conditions" appeared on the office notice board of a Burnley cotton mill in 1852.

1 Godliness, cleanliness and punctuality are the necessities of a good business.
2 This firm has reduced the hours of work, and the clerical staff will now only have to be present between the hours of 7 am and 6 pm on weekdays.
3 Daily prayers will be held each morning in the main office. The clerical staff will be present.
4 Clothing must be of a sober nature. The clerical staff will not disport themselves in raiment of bright colours, nor will they wear hose, unless in good repair.
5 Overshoes and top-coats may not be worn in the office, but neck scarves and headwear may be worn in inclement weather.
6 A stove is provided for the benefit of the clerical staff. Coal and wood must be kept in the locker. It is recommended that each member of the clerical staff bring 4 pounds of coal each day during cold weather.
7 No member of the clerical staff may leave the room without permission from Mr. Rogers. The calls of nature are permitted and clerical staff may use the garden below the second gate. This area must be kept in good order.
8 No talking is allowed during business hours.
9 The craving of tobacco, wines or spirits is a human weakness and, as such, is forbidden to all members of the clerical staff.
10 Now that the hours of business have been drastically reduced, the partaking of food is allowed between 11.30 am and noon, but work will not, on any account, cease.
11 Members of the clerical staff will provide their own pens. A new sharpener is available, on application to Mr. Rogers.
12 Mr. Rogers will nominate a senior clerk to be responsible for the cleanliness of the main office and the private office, and all boys and juniors will report to him 40 minutes before prayers, and will remain after closing hours for similar work. Brushes, brooms, scrubbers and soap are provided by the owners.
13 The new increased weekly wages are as hereunder detailed: Junior boys (up to 11 years) 1s 4d, Boys (to 14 years) 2s 1d, Juniors 4s 8d, Junior clerks 8s 7d, Clerks 10s 9d, Senior clerks (after 15 years with owners) 21s.

The owners recognise the generosity of the new Labour Laws, but will expect a great rise in output of work to compensate for these near Utopian conditions. *Shades of Maggie!*

Eulogy

I wasn't sure how to start this. Five or ten minutes to encapsulate Grandma. The truth is it is an impossible task to begin. So, I'm just going to mention the things that come to my mind-snapshots from my memory-that are Grandma. To be honest, I will be amazed if these are not some of the memories of us all. Sitting on Grandmas' knee on her rocking chair, singing one of the many songs, lilac trees, big rock candy mountain, there was an old woman who swallowed a fly or listened as she regaled stories of her youth and family life.

How many of us liked nothing better than to sit quietly and listen to the little match girl-Grandma in her rocking chair, always at the centre?

Then there was her baking, never just one plain old cake for Alice but a selection, from coconut sponge to meat and potato and lemon meringue pies. All left to cool on the back step. And which one of us doesn't have vivid memories of making the Christmas cakes? Chopping the almonds and glacé cherries and constantly trying not to get caught eating them. Reminded every time it was the syrup that gave the Christmas cake its dark colour, not the treacle. Nothing ever weighed out, just how her mother had always done-in grandma's words, a tribute to her memory.

Unfortunately, this is one gene Grandma failed to pass on to most of us! Now wash day-hard enough without an automatic washing machine-but even though just the thought of the task must have made her tired. She knew the enjoyment her Grandchildren got from using the posser, tub and scrubbing board. So, it would all be hauled out and what seemed like a daylong undertaking began. Even after all this hard work -the ironing was always done immediately- no stuffing in baskets and cupboards for grandma-everything -socks, pants, hankies ironed and hung on the pulley-the best pillowcases always put to the front. Lots of smiles and laughter, with everyone, left soaked in the process.

Grandma was a knowledgeable and dignified woman. As a child, she would read anything she could get her hands on, even if it were only the racing post. In later years, writing expressed Grandma's love of words in her writing-her vivid descriptions of People, events, emotions, and observations from her life. Allowing us all the great privilege of an insight into times and life's gone by. However, we all know grandma could also have a mischievous side to her. Who doesn't remember being chased around by her with her false teeth? Or pinned to the floor with Grandma sitting on top of you when you had been bickering? Then the great hilarity of the notorious flee that flew past our door. I'm sure you're all thinking of something very similar right now. These instances were some of the things that made Grandma so special.

When having such a huge family, children, Sheila, Gordon, Ann and Stanley, Grandchildren, Great Grandchildren and even a great great, Grandchild-she still could make every one of us seem unique to her. Giving all of us warm, happy memories of our childhoods will, in turn, be reflected in our own children's memories. Something that grandma instilled in all of us the most precious gifts in life -family and children -present and past-they make us the people we are.

Very few of us were lucky enough to meet Grandad Lambert, but we all felt close to him through Grandma. As close a connection as we could have had, had we spent time with him all our lives, I'm sure if I asked you to put your hand up if you could put your socks on like Grandad Lambert, there would be countless arms in the air. This example is as good a point as any to start drawing to an end-Lambert the love of Grandma's life -sadly, had to leave Grandma. In December 1966, near his end, he said, 'I'm going to die,

Alice, and I want you to promise not to remarry, you see I love you, and I'll wait for you' well, she certainly bloody made him wait a long time.

But now they're both where they would want to be back together again and reunited once more with their youngest son Stanley and their Grandson Mark. To finish off, I'll read some of Grandma's words that I think to say it all.

"As long as I remember, I have a glow, a brightness within, something that made each day worth living. I tried to reason the why and the wherefore, now, I believe I am beginning to understand-it was love -belonging to a happy family and the awareness of being loved."

And by God was she loved by all of us. Night God bless auld flea!

Alice Cook, a Lancashire Lass

About the Author

Alice Eckersley Cook. Born 21st January 1915, in Atherton, Lancashire. Alice was born into abject poverty but with a wealth of love. She was a working-class woman and was proud of it.

She had a thirst for education. She was a fighter and survived a bout of tuberculosis at a young age. Alice went on to have a family of four children and many grandchildren. All were made to feel special.

Alice lost her husband to cancer in her fifties, this saw the start of her writings as she documented the last heart-breaking few months of her husband Lambert's life. Along with the love of her family, her writing would become one of the things that sustained Alice in the years after losing Lambert.

This passion for writing left a legacy recording her beliefs in equality and the working class. Alice was an intelligent, self-taught woman, she had an indomitable spirit, she defied the norm, she was an activist, a trade unionist and championed the working-class struggle and was not scared to call out injustice.

This book offers an insight into the life of Alice- a Lancashire lass- it not only illustrates an historic awareness of the struggles of ordinary people, but also demonstrates the talents and creativity of an individual who loves her family deeply, whilst still grappling with the challenges of everyday life.

Printed in Great Britain
by Amazon

18657506R10078